Teen Love ™

ON FRIENDSHIP

ON FRIENDSHIP

A Book for Teenagers

KIMBERLY KIRBERGER

Chicken Soup for the Teenage Soul series

with Colin Mortensen
from MTV's *Real World Hawaii*

HCI
TEENS
Health Communications, Inc.
Deerfield Beach, Florida

www.hci-online.com
www.love4teens.com

We would like to acknowledge the many publishers and individuals who granted us permission to reprint the cited material. (Note: The stories that were penned anonymously, that are in the public domain or that were written by Kimberly Kirberger are not included in this listing.)

All material in boxed text by Colin Mortensen is reprinted by permission of Colin Mortensen. ©2000 Colin Mortensen.

Be. Reprinted by permission of Aja Ofte. ©2000 Aja Ofte.

Lost in a Sea of Faces, To Hide in Fear and *Foolish Girl.* Reprinted by permission of Rebecca Woolf. ©2000 Rebecca Woolf.

What You Do Today. Reprinted by permission of Becca Mustard. ©2000 Becca Mustard.

(continued on page 379)

Library of Congress Cataloging-in-Publication Data

Kirberger, Kimberly, date.
   On friendship : book for teenagers / Kimberly Kirberger.
      p.   cm. — (Teen love series)
   ISBN 1-55874-815-6
     1. Teenagers—Life skills guides—Juvenile literature.
   2. Friendship—Juvenile literature. 3. Teenagers—Conduct of life—
Juvenile literature.   4. Interpersonal relations—Juvenile literature.
   [1. Friendship. 2. Interpersonal relations.]   I. Title.

HQ796.K476 2000
302.3'4—dc21   00-058167

©2000 Kimberly Kirberger

ISBN 1-55874-815-6

Publisher: Health Communications, Inc.
                  3201 S.W. 15th Street
                  Deerfield Beach, FL 33442-8190

Cover and inside book design by Lawna Patterson Oldfield

With love I dedicate this book to my son, Jesse. Your kindness and humor make you a great friend.

With love I also dedicate this book to the many teens who I am lucky enough to call friend. (Many of them are really Jesse's friends, but are sweet enough to let me call them friend, too.) I love you guys: Christine, Lia, James, Ashley, Cory, Hayley, Madison, Lily, Nico, Caitlin, Jenny, Amber, Una, Taylor, Hannah, Alex, Charlotte, Vanessa, Cary.

With love also to my very cool nephew, Christopher.

I am so grateful to have a life that is filled with teenagers' trust and love.

Contents

3. What Is Friendship?

4. Challenges in Friendship

5. Making Friends

6. Cliques, Groups and Popularity

7. Friends and Lovers

8. Jealousy, Hurt and Betrayal

9. Friends in Trouble

10. Growing Apart

11. The Best of Friendship

 # Acknowledgments

I am grateful to be able to have my work be something that I love so completely. Every time I am able to help a teen, gain the trust of a teen or simply have a conversation with a teen, I feel totally blessed. For all this I am very thankful.

I am very appreciative of the love and support I receive from my husband, John, who continually makes me laugh. Our "friendship" is strengthened every time we laugh together—usually at ourselves. John, you are brilliant, talented, funny and kind, and I am lucky to have you to pick on and love . . . so much.

My unconditional love goes to my son, Jesse, who is so amazing and has taught me so much. At this moment you are fifteen, and Jesse, you have already surpassed my greatest expectations of what a son should be. It is all gravy from here. Seriously, you have the kindest heart, the sharpest mind and the funniest sense of humor. You are multitalented and humble enough to want me to stop . . . but there's more! Your band is great, I love your girlfriend and you are the best son I could have ever wished for. Thank you. I love you.

I love and thank my parents for everything, including putting up with my freak-outs each time we moved, and

I had to leave all my friends behind and make new ones. I thank you both for teaching me about hard work, being kind, making a difference and going for my dreams.

My brother Jack is my best friend. Jack believed in me when I didn't believe in myself and always told me I could do it. It was because of his faith in me that I was able to do the first book, and he continues to support me in ways that are magical. I have always looked up to him because he is my oldest brother and because he always excelled at everything he did. It has been really great to have our friendship become more equal, and to realize that we each would choose the other as a friend even if we weren't related. I have so much respect for who you are, Jack. Your generosity and your ability to inspire others make you unique. I love you dearly and am so grateful to have you as my friend. You've even gotten very funny.

My dear friend Tasha is so sweet and so smart and so good at what she does. Her guidance, encouragement, sense of humor and amazing skill are the reasons I am able to do these books. This book was really a huge effort for me, and it was Tasha who always reassured me and pushed me to keep going. She took my words and made them into sentences and more than once made me look a lot smarter than I really was. (Who wouldn't love that?) I love you, Tasha, and I consider you one of my dearest friends.

Then there is Mitch. Mitch is perfect. He is the vice president of I.A.M. 4 Teens, Inc., and he keeps the whole show together. Mitch is involved in every step of the process, and he has the absolute best work ethic I have ever seen. He works hard because he cares that the books get completed, the Web site continues to support thousands of teens, all the employees of I.A.M. 4 Teens are happy and productive, and on and on. Mitch, I am so grateful. Thank you from the bottom of my heart.

Nina Palais is our den mother. She is one of those people in whose presence one can't help but feel nurtured. Nina is the president of the Teen Letter Project. She makes sure that all the letters get answered, that all the submissions are read carefully and given over for consideration to the appropriate book and, most of all, she makes sure that the teens on staff are well taken care of. She also is the mother of two of my favorite teenagers, Ashley and Taylor, and she has done an amazing job of raising them. You go, girl!!!!

Thank-you to Kelly Harrington. Kelly is the rights and permissions director, and because of her hard work and diligence we are able to use some great stories, poems and excerpts. I thank you, Kelly, for being such a hard worker and for being so dedicated. You are deeply appreciated.

My thanks to Lisa Vasquez, my personal assistant, for all that she does. There are days where Lisa is asked to run around doing twenty different things at once, and she always, always has a smile on her face and a pleasant attitude. I really appreciate you, Lisa, and all the things you do; and I love your smile.

To all the teens who have staffed the Teen Letter Project, my deepest appreciation. You have done an excellent job of providing support to thousands of teens around the world. It's been a joy to work with and get to know all of you: Dawn Geer, Lisa Rothbard, Lindsay Ross, Elliott Hallmark, Marc Robins, Rose Lannutti, Christine Alvarez, Vanessa Little, Arianna Axelrod, Jane Cary McCormick, Ashley Fisher, Christine Kalinowski.

Our Web-site monitors have done a great job with the upkeep of our Web site. My gratitude goes to: Mariana Bernasconi, Michael Christian Smith, Laura Bauer, Bernadette Donovan.

A very, very special thank-you to the teenagers who helped me with this book by coming to my house every Sunday and sharing their deepest feelings and thoughts about friendship with me. I never could have done this without this group of teens being so open about what things were hard for them and what information they felt teens could benefit from hearing. The best thing of all was the day we discussed what each person appreciated about each other in the room. The depth and intensity of love these guys have for each other made it all clear for me. I knew from that moment that this book would have a very special element within its pages, and it does. So, from the bottom of my heart, I thank each and every one of you for sharing your heart so that other teens could benefit from your insights and wisdom. You guys are so amazing and I love you all very much: Ashley Fisher, Emma Bates, Liz Stein, Caitlin Owens, Hannah Hubble, Lily Lamden, Vanessa Little, Jenny Sharaf, Amber Brockman, Una Maslesa, Charlotte Grubb, Hayley

Gibson, Jane Cary McCormick.

Also many thanks to Cory Bergamini, Madison Marek, Alex Davis, Michael Lipkin, Nico Aguayo, Lisa Gumenick, Lisa Rothbard, Bree Abel, Hana Ivanhoe, Jessie Braun and all the other teens who have inspired me.

Thank you, Peter Vegso, for your continued support of the work that I am doing for teens. Living up to your nickname for me of "Teen Queen" has been a challenge and a joy. An extra-special thank-you for your commitment to and support of this book.

A warm thank-you to Lisa Drucker for her inspiring nature and talented editing skills. It has been a joy to work with you, Lisa. You are an amazing woman, and I appreciate your friendship.

Thanks to Susan Tobias for her skilled editing work and her attention to detail. Susan, you have been a pleasure to work with.

Thanks to Larissa Hise Henoch, Lawna Patterson Oldfield and Lisa Camp for their hard work on the artwork for this book.

Thanks to Kim Weiss and Maria Konicki at HCI for their talented publicity efforts. You guys are a strong and spirited team dedicated to making these books a success. I appreciate everything you have done for me.

Thanks to Sharon Much for her calm brilliance and all she's done to get the word out there.

Thanks also to Randee Feldman for her talented marketing work and to Terry Burke for his tenacious efforts in sales.

Thank you, Karen Ornstein and Kelly Maragni, for being so good at what you do, and for your support of this project.

Patty Aubery, I wish I could clone you and have one of you here with me at all times. Instead, I have to be happy with small doses of your genius, your great personality, and your unbelievable ability to know so much, be so sharp and so funny at the same time. Unfortunately, you are a one-of-a-kinder.

To Kim Foley, the sweetest girlfriend I have ever had, you are the best. You are my angel and I can only hope that I am yours.

Lia Gay, I have watched you grow up and now I am watching you grow. You have always been brilliant, beautiful, articulate, talented and simply one of my favorite people. I am now watching you become responsible, grateful, mature, wise beyond your years and in love. You have always brought me great joy, but now you bring even more. You are a wonderful friend, a wonderful goddaughter, a wonderful person, and I love you very much.

Colin Mortensen: What can I say? I admired you as the guy I watched every Tuesday night on MTV's *Real World Hawaii*. I was often amazed at the integrity you demonstrated while still being a fun-loving and gorgeous guy. Then I got to meet you and I was pleasantly surprised that the real you was even better than the "Real World" you. The thing that makes me happiest is that you and your friendship just keep getting better with time. (I'll refrain from comparing you to a fine wine.) I am truly grateful to have you as a friend and a partner. I am also thankful to have had something to do with what I know will be a very bright future for you, as both a writer and a gift to the teens who will read your words and get to know you better as well.

Last, but certainly not least, I want to thank YOU, the reader of these books. I appreciate the support, the letters of thanks and the trust you place in me. It is because of readers like you that I am able to continue to do these books for teens, and for that there are no sufficient words to express my gratitude. I thank you from the deepest place in my heart.

Kimberly Kirberger

Mom and Dad, thanks for always believing in me.

Ryan, I love you.

Max, "Colin all done."

Tro, Eiffel Tower.

Mike, Whatever.

Casey, Italy.

Dave, Alta Bates.

Matt, "Sweet Home Berryessa."

Kelly, ASU.

Glenn Morgan, for your vision, your intelligence, and, most of all, for giving me a shot.

Jeff Meshel, for believing and for being so damn nice.

Kim Kirberger, for having so much faith and heart.

Colin Mortensen

"We have no secrets and no privacy! They can see and hear everything we do! I'm telling you guys, we're the new cast of the *Real World!*"

Reprinted by permission of Randy Glasbergen.

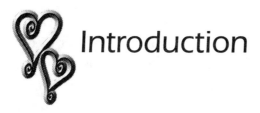 Introduction

---

♥

I had a friend once.

Jesse Kirberger

Friendship is such a huge thing. When I first set out to write and compile this book I knew it would be challenging. I knew that especially in adolescence, friendship can cause great happiness and great sorrow. I knew that there were many definitions of friendship and that it means something a little different to everyone. I knew all these things, but I didn't know that I was about to embark on such a huge challenge in both my writing career and my personal life.

I have seen the beauty of the human spirit and the sacredness involved when hearts come together in friendship, and I have also seen the dark side and the pain caused when we forget that our actions affect others and that to hurt another is to hurt ourselves. I have come to believe that if we can learn to be a friend to ourselves and to others then we will have achieved what we were put on this earth to do.

I have learned that being a friend and having friends is an ongoing process and each time we are hurt or disappointed, it is an opportunity to learn something new. The key is to enjoy the friendships we have and, even if they don't work out, keep ourselves and our hearts open so that we can experience the great joy that friendship can bring.

The joy that comes from being there for someone, from laughing and sharing with another person, from knowing what the other person is thinking without a word being spoken, and feeling safe to be all that we are, is a joy that cannot be topped. The peace and happiness that comes from having and being a good friend is the absolute best and certainly worth the challenges friendship can present.

In this book, we will look at many aspects of friendship. We will read stories of best friends, friendships gone wrong and of friendships that have simply grown apart. We will read stories of friends who have helped each other, cheered each other up and in some cases literally saved one another's life. We will hear about friends becoming lovers and lovers becoming friends. Teens who thought they would never have a friend will tell us about how that changed and someone who thought they were better than others will share being humbled by an experience that showed them differently.

From the thousands of letters I have received and from the friendship forum on our Web site, I have read about most, if not all, the problems that plague teens in the area of friendship. I have done my best to include the most common ones. As is true with all the books in this series, the goal is first and foremost for you to see you are not alone. The stories will tell of situations similar to ones you have experienced and in some cases will go on to share how a particular problem was resolved. The poetry in the book will help put into words the thoughts and feelings you have for a friend or the pain you have felt when a friend betrayed you. Throughout the book Colin and I have shared our wisdom and thoughts with you. Our hope is that our words will inspire you or simply remind you of what you already know to be true.

I hope that this book comforts you and guides you in many ways. Remember, as always, happiness and friendship are things you do have control over. The more you do to achieve joy with yourself and others, the more joy you will have.

Good luck and enjoy the journey.

One

Being Yourself!

Be

Be intelligent,
Be happy,
Be adorable on occasion,
Be flirtatious,
Be sophisticated,
Be charitable,
Be bold,
Be strong,
Be pleasant,
Be grateful for being,
Be your own person,
But whatever you choose to be today,
Be yourself!

Aja Ofte

A Journey to Self-Discovery

I believe that these, your teen years, are the years when the journey to self-discovery begins. Those who have the desire and the courage to embark on this journey with the full intent of getting to know themselves will be the ones who find the most happiness in the years to come.

—KIMBERLY KIRBERGER

Being Yourself!

♥
―――――――――――――

I strongly believe you should
never judge people by how they look.
The only thing that matters is
what's on the inside.

Nick of the Backstreet Boys

Friends come together to learn and grow with one
another, to lighten each other's loads and brighten each
other's days. Our friends can have a tremendous impact
on our lives. They are our teachers and our guides, our
support systems and our cheerleaders. It is a big responsibility to be a good friend. So it is very important to
come into a friendship with a solid sense of who we are—
we should be able to give our friend our best, most
authentic self. It is only by being real with our friends
that we can truly give the gift of our friendship. Our
friends will enjoy our company so much more if we can
be ourselves in their presence. The payoff for us is

enormous. We are assured that we are loved for ourselves rather than someone we are pretending to be and, because of that, we are able to be completely at ease.

But how do we know when we are truly being ourselves? How do we learn to be ourselves? Being yourself is a process and not a destination, and there are steps that you can take to start being yourself.

Begin by asking yourself the question, *Who am I?*

- What are my values? What do I believe in and what do I consider important?
- What do I like? What are my hobbies or interests? How do I like to spend my time? What type of movies, books or TV shows do I like?
- What is my personality? What do I care about? What are some words I would use to describe myself?

When we don't know the answer to these basic questions, we run the risk of taking on identities that are not truly ours in order to please others. We've all had the experience of taking on an identity that is not really our own. Even if we won the approval and acknowledgment of the people we were trying to impress, it is a hollow victory. We end up feeling lonely and empty when we aren't being true to ourselves.

Another way to know ourselves is to know our *boundaries*. It is important to know our limits—what we will and won't do, what we need or don't need, and what we want or don't want. Boundaries are the lines we draw around ourselves to protect us; they are our borders. It is that voice that tells us, "No, this doesn't feel right to me," or the knowledge that we deserve better. We will be challenged many times either to do what's easy and popular or to do what's right. It isn't always easy to stand up for yourself when it isn't the popular stance, but you only need to do this one time to know that the way in which it empowers you makes it totally worthwhile.

In friendships, if we don't communicate our boundaries to others we can resent the other person for sapping our time and energy. We can become irritated and even angry with another person when we aren't true to ourselves. This could lead to hurting that person's feelings unintentionally. We end up blaming our friends for not "seeing" or "knowing somehow" that they were asking too much of us. If we can take responsibility for saying what our needs are, we can avoid situations that result in resentment. The key is to be real clear about what our needs are, and to express our limits before any bad feelings build up. This positive action on our parts can make us feel much better about ourselves.

Another aspect of being ourselves is accepting *all* parts of ourselves: the good, the bad and the ugly. This doesn't mean it's fine to exhibit such negative behaviors as lying and stealing and simply write it off as, "Hey, I'm not perfect." We should always resist any temptation to behave in a way that hurts others and ourselves. But it is important to realize that we all have shadow sides to ourselves. Nobody is perfect. We all have feelings of envy, judgment, jealousy, guilt, anger and fear. These feelings are just part of the human experience. The important thing is not to beat ourselves up for these feelings but to have compassion for ourselves in those moments.

If we condemn our faults instead of trying to understand them, we won't grow and learn. Most importantly, each time we accept our own limitations we can more fully begin to accept the limitations of other people. This is one of the most important factors in being a good friend.

As with everything, being yourself is a journey. It is never complete. We don't wake up one day and proclaim that we are now "ourselves." The treasure is in the learning, not in the final destination.

Lost in a Sea of Faces

REBECCA WOOLF

My senior year I was crowned Homecoming Queen, an honor given to me by my friends and peers. As the banner rolled down the side of the gymnasium with my name written in huge block letters, my vision blurred and the past surfaced. The sea of faces cheering in the stands faded away, and I was left alone with my past.

It was sixth-grade promotion, the biggest transition I had faced, and I shook in my new white high heels. I was awkward in elementary school, harassed for my buckteeth and flat chest, tormented by the boys for being ugly, and mocked by the girls for being meek. All I ever wanted was to be accepted. And as I stood there looking out at the sea of familiar faces, I wondered if I ever would be.

That summer was one of extreme growth for me. I grew into my awkward self, finding a voice and a new release: writing. I had kept a journal for years before, but now I had made it a daily routine. I expressed my fears, doubts,

worries and dreams in my denim-covered notebook;
through poetry, through prose and through everyday
ideas. Through writing, I found a friend—myself.

On the first day of junior high, I stared into the bathroom mirror. "All right, Becca," I said, "whatever happens,
happens, don't be afraid." I smiled to myself, kissed my
mom good-bye and scurried to the bus stop. That first day
of school was inspiring. I had a great schedule with nice
teachers and plenty of new acquaintances. As the year
progressed, my friends increased and my awkward
appearance melted away. I no longer spent lunch in the
bathroom or did all of my assignments alone. The boys
who made fun of me a year ago were now asking me to the
movies, and the girls who had once ignored me were sitting with me at lunch. I was accepted. The years passed.

I was popular and therefore stuck with an isolated
image I didn't quite know how to handle. I hid every flaw,
every feeling, and every insecurity behind makeup and
smiles that weren't real. I didn't understand why I felt so
inaccessible. Popularity wasn't supposed to be lonely.

I wrote more and more, hiding my pain and confusion
in the pages of my journal. I didn't want my peers to
know that I was human, and therefore I didn't open up
to anyone. My true colors were deep within me, scribbled
in the darkness of my soul. I forgot how it felt to be on
the other side, so when my friends ridiculed and made
fun of others, I stood back in disregard. I became one of
the girls who used to make me cry, and yet I didn't want to
break away. I depended on them and not myself. I didn't
want to be my own best friend, because then I might lose

my place, my identity. I didn't understand that I already had it.

I spoke at our junior high graduation, preparing the class for a new change: high school. As I stood before my friends and acquaintances, I welled up with tears. I didn't like the girl I had become; I was lost.

High school was the same. I still stuck by my friends, but I needed to find myself. I watched them struggle with their own identities. I watched them hide behind the same smiles. I watched them ridicule and mock, in spite of their own insecurities and confusion. And finally I had enough. One day at lunch, I broke down.

Lunch was a time for gossip and "discussion." Who was dating whom, and who was wearing what. I was at the point where I didn't really care, and so I ate my lunch without the usual commentary. "Becca, what's your deal?"

"My *deal?*" That was it; I backlashed. I began yelling hysterically. I told them how sick I was of all the talk, the walk, the image. I told them that I wanted to be real, that I hurt, that I was confused, just like everybody else. I told them about elementary school, and how I would come home every day crying, because I wasn't accepted, because I wasn't good enough. I told them that I hurt, and felt like I wasn't supposed to, and that I wrote poetry and hid it in fear of revealing part of me that no one knew existed. I opened up every pore and detoxed right there in the middle of lunch.

Silence. No one knew what to say. It didn't matter; they didn't need to say anything. They felt the same as I did; they were just afraid. I knew—I saw it in their eyes.

From that point on, things were different. Slowly, I drifted. I opened myself up to different kinds of people and realized that I had more in common with those outside the social loop. I became more involved with my own interests, I became more self-assured. I found myself again. I found the best friend I had forgotten was inside of me, and she gave me the courage to run with my individuality. I wrote poetry and shared it. I hosted the TV news show at school and other school events. I was respected, not by a few, but by everyone. I stood up for the little girl who was pushed around, for she was part of who I was now.

The faces reappeared, and I felt myself smile. I made it. I looked out into the audience, and for once I felt understood. I had friends who cared about me, friends of the past and friends of the present. Friendships that had drifted in and out and in again. But most important, I had myself, and in her honor I wore that crown.

"I've gotta be me . . . but I can't help thinking
someone else would be more qualified!"

Reprinted by permission of Randy Glasbergen.

What You Do Today

BECCA MUSTARD

Break away from all that is real.
Forget how you think, forget how you feel.
Live life today, forget things gone by.
Live your own truth and not the world's lie.
Create a life of living, be spontaneous and brave.
Go off the beaten path, find your own road to pave.
For if you live life for you and you alone,
You'll be your own master and create your own throne.
The world around may tell you what to do or say,
But tomorrow is too worrisome; concentrate on today.
Things may have gone wrong in the days of the past,
But he who looks at yesterday always finishes last.
Learn from your mistakes and move on twice as wise.
Help those less fortunate, smile at those you despise.
And once your life is over, once your journey's done,
You will know you ran the race, and you will know
     you've won.
For yesterday is hopeless and tomorrow's far away,
But in the end it will matter what you do today.

Being Yourself

Being yourself has to do with being comfortable in your own skin. It has to do with knowing yourself and liking yourself. Often what keeps us from knowing ourselves is trying to ignore the parts of ourselves that aren't perfect.

—KIMBERLY KIRBERGER

Mirrors

One of the best ways to learn about yourself is to see yourself through your friends' eyes. Our friends are like mirrors who reflect back to us our good and bad traits.

—KIMBERLY KIRBERGER

A Short Kind of Death

SILAS LESNICK

Our actions determine who we are and, in turn, who we are determines our actions. Life is only worthwhile so long as we are happy to live it. One thing I've learned is that if we lose track of who we are, we lose track of where we're headed in life. I once had a friend who lost track. He ended up forgetting who he was in an experience that would change us both forever.

For five years, we were best friends. We shared a love of comic books, action figures and *Star Wars*. We threw a going-away party for our local comic book store when it closed. We were inseparable, he and I, and there was a time when it seemed nothing could tear us apart.

And then one day, it all began to change. Slowly and gradually, he turned away from it all. He stopped reading comics and watching movies, and we grew further and further apart. He sacrificed his identity for a darker future. He became involved with drugs, and I watched while, over a period of about a year, he degraded from a creative, straight-A student to someone who was failing all his classes from skipping too much school. All the while, I could do nothing but ignore the fact that I was losing my friend.

I realized after the fact that I had let him slip away. I trusted he would find his own way back and pull through it alone. I abandoned him when my help could have made all the difference. I realize now that one can't always expect things to turn out all right. Unless we take action and shape our present, we must accept whatever future we arrive at. Perhaps if I had spoken out and forced him to realize where he was headed, he would have tried to change paths.

But I also realize that I couldn't allow what happened to him happen to me, and it's scary to think how easily it could have. Looking back, I'm determined to learn from his mistakes. The last thing I want is to abandon who I am. My identity makes me happy. I look at myself and know that no matter what I have to go through, I've defined myself and that makes me appreciate life. I have confidence in my individuality, and the last thing I want is to serve as a haunting reminder to someone else.

A Strange Paradox

One of the stranger paradoxes in the world of friendship is that sometimes the more people we surround ourselves with, the lonelier we feel. I think it has something to do with people expecting or wanting us to act or be a certain way. When we surround ourselves with people we don't quite know or completely trust, our real, authentic self tends to hide out. We don't feel safe so we enter into a mode of self-protection. If we express our true, unique selves we run the risk of other people judging us or hurting us. This is why we can feel so lonely and isolated—we yearn for someone to see us as we really are.

—KIMBERLY KIRBERGER

Black Fans

JUDY NEE

We are our best selves when we
are being our true selves.

Kimberly Kirberger

My mother is feeding me her Chinese food and keeps stuffing my plate with more and more octopus legs and chow mein, rice and fried vegetables. The oil drips from her spoon, slowly, as if it were savoring each moment of its descent. "Stop!" I keep telling her. "Stop!" But she continues to fill a big soup goblet with another heap of eggplant. I look her straight in the eye and finally say in Chinese, *"Byao."*

She doesn't understand; I tug on her sleeve, push the spoon away, like a weapon, and say no again.

The same dream, each time. It's never an emphatic *no* of anger; rather, it is always one of helplessness. In American magazines, I read stories about first-generation Asian-Americans, and I know I'm one of them, but I just can't see it. I find myself trying to say something incredibly profound to my mother, to tell her how I feel when I'm having a fight with my best friend, but at the most important part, I can't remember the words that will say everything that I need to tell her. It's like finding yourself suddenly mute, completely frustrated at what you can't express. She accepts my phrases of English words sandwiched in Chinese idioms, but I feel like I don't belong anywhere.

When I was eleven, she dragged my whole family to an art school's talent show. The principal was from Shanghai and had established a school for people like my mother who don't want to lose the Chinese culture to hot dogs and hamburgers. We met my relatives in the front of the auditorium, my eldest aunt expressing to me for the nth time how dark I am. "Have you been in the sun all summer?" she cried, and hastily grabbed one of the porcelain Chinese girls from the school to show me their wonderful color. "This girl is so nice," she said, and glazed her hand under her model's chin. I responded to her in Chinese that I'm naturally this dark, but she grabbed hold of my mother and frantically asked, "Why does she speak like an American?"

My family and I finally filed into the showroom, where the curtains were bright red, to signify luck, for the show. Dancers streamed onto the stage. Two of the girls in the front led the rest. Their pale-blue outfits, like the silk suits you see in movies, loosely fit their bodies. Each of them held a black fan with the word "Fortune" sprawled across the folds. They twisted and turned, snapping their fans open and closed very slowly to the beat of a lone drummer, the sound pulsating with each step they took. It looked glorious, a dance that was strong, yet cultivated and delicate at the same time.

I glanced over to my mother who I imagined was wishing that I would be one of those dark-haired princesses. She was beaming, obviously, but looked straight ahead.

During the entire show, she never once looked to see whether I regretted my American television or American ideals, nor did she mention how proud she was of those girls.

It's like that joke about what came first, the chicken or the egg. I don't know what came first, Chinese or American. No matter how much I speak with the perfect American accent and forget every word that passes through Chinese lips, I'm still that damned foreigner. But I am striking each beat, opening and closing my fan, with that lone drummer, with every breath of Chinese and American knowledge I know.

In my nightmares, I still cry "stop" to my mother to her second helpings of hearty Chinese food, and once in a while she looks up and says in English, "I understand."

Myself

KAYLA JOANNA WOODS

Part of me is dazzling purple—
  energetic and sprightly,
  sharp and keen,
  laughing at my friends and enjoying their reactions.
But deep inside there's another part,
  pale blue, like a blue bonnet hiding under
    itself—
  timid and uncertain,
  apprehensive and nervous,
  scared to death when asked out.
Yet they're both very real,
  and they're both me.

"I hate to argue with my parents,
but that's what we do best!"

Sculpting Yourself

Part of being a teenager is discovering who we are. It is not something that happens overnight. We test ourselves by seeing how we respond to different situations. We try different styles and a different look until we find something that feels right for us. We test out different value systems to see which ones feel good and which ones don't.

The thing to remember is that you are sculpting you. In order to do that, you have to make mistakes. You have to try things on for size. Many of those things will clearly be you—and many of those things won't.

This is why some teenagers have struggles with their parents. You have to figure out for yourself what is important to you and what your values are. You may go through a period where you disregard everything your parents have taught you. But as time passes, you will see that it isn't about accepting everything they taught you or rejecting all of it, it is about making the things you agree with your own and lovingly setting aside the things you don't.

Just remember that when you do make discoveries about yourself, don't shy away from them. Keep them as yours and know that each time another discovery is made you are closer to knowing yourself.

—KIMBERLY KIRBERGER

♥

Nothing Wrong with Being Me

If my friends are only comfortable with the one side of me that I consistently show them, then maybe they don't really know the whole me. It is my job to be strong enough and secure enough to show them that I am different people at different times.

What's wrong with being unpredictable? Whether it's a desire to be quiet or a need to express a deeply felt opinion or perspective about the world, I have to work to give myself the freedom to be me. Even if I don't always know exactly who that person is. Even if others may not like or accept the new "me." My greatest responsibility is to myself and to my personal growth.

—COLIN MORTENSEN

Being Judged

Every single one of us has had to endure being judged for something about ourselves that does not deserve judgment—too tall, too skinny, too fat, not pretty, too pretty, talks funny, acts different and so on. In fact, more often than not we are the ones doing the judging. As long as there are things about ourselves that we do not accept, we are vulnerable to the judgment of others. It is important to remember that when others are being overly critical of us it has very little to do with us and a lot to do with how they feel about themselves. When we learn to truly accept ourselves, the judgments and the cruelty of others will roll off our backs.

People who put other people down do it because they feel bad about themselves. This is not just something people say to make you feel better. It is absolutely true. If we feel bad about ourselves, we see ugliness everywhere. If we feel good about ourselves, we see goodness everywhere.

—KIMBERLY KIRBERGER

You Want to Be Different

ALISON DANKMEYER

Expansions, reductions, pulls, tucks and lifts
The things we will do to our most precious gifts
But the fad and the fashion will change when you wake
To the mold you have melted but not for your sake
Too straight, too crooked, too short or too flat
Too round, too square, too bony, too fat
Lips too thin and hips too wide
Too often the truth gets left behind
Too little, too many, too much to say
Too timid, too quiet, or too loud today
Hair too dark and eyes too small
Too fair, too weak, too plump, too tall
Too proud, too crippled, too wicked, too old
A mind too slow, a heart too cold
Too tempted, too worried, too evil, too nice
Too willing to change for too big a price
A dress too tight, and jeans too blue
Too frizzy, too faded, too common, too few

Feet too big and arms too long
Too skinny, too mean, too bold and too strong
Too many thoughts and too many tears
Too many scares and too many fears
Too curvy, too wavy, too pointed, too kind
Too soon to accept, too long to unwind
Too hard, too soft, too sleazy, too bright
Too trusting, too shallow, too cheerful, too right
The picture of perfect is not a set thing
It's an album you look through, a note that you sing
Being too ignorant, deaf and too blind
You don't seem to want to be one of a kind
Too hard to be striving, too easy to blame
Instead of a difference, you'll end up the same.

Express Our True Selves

We are complex beings. Why not acknowledge it? Why not celebrate it? Why not have the courage to show it? We all lose out when we try to whittle ourselves down to the expectations of others. The best thing to do is just relax and express our true selves in whatever way seems right at the moment. As long as we're not hurting others, or ourselves, we should be able to show all sides of our personalities.

—COLIN MORTENSEN

Ways to Be Yourself and Love Yourself

KIMBERLY KIRBERGER

1. Celebrate your uniqueness.
2. Know what you like and don't like.
3. Like what you see when you look in the mirror.
4. Every now and then, dress exactly the way you like, instead of dressing like your friends.
5. Think about things that make you happy.
6. Think with your heart.
7. Do something creative by yourself.
8. Pick one day a week that is "your day" to do what you need.
9. Do something athletic without competing.
10. Read a great book.
11. Do something kind for someone else.
12. Do something kind and don't let anyone know you did it.
13. When someone compliments you, let it in and say, "Thanks!"

14. Plant something and watch it grow.
15. Spend some time alone doing nothing.
16. Make your room your own. Decorate it, put pictures of your friends or what makes you happy everywhere.
17. Forgive yourself for everything you've ever done and start clean.
18. Dream big dreams for yourself and know your dreams can come true.
19. Say one nice thing to yourself every day.
20. Start each day by being grateful.

Two

Being Your Own Best Friend

Love yourself first and
everything else falls into line.
You really have to love yourself
first to get anything done
in this world.

Lucille Ball

Intention

So much of being our own best friend is the <u>intention</u> behind our actions. It is a choice we make to treat ourselves with tenderness.

—KIMBERLY KIRBERGER

Know, Accept and Love Yourself

I am sure there is nothing in life you will ever do that is more important than first, getting to know yourself and second, accepting and loving what you find.

—KIMBERLY KIRBERGER

Being Your Own Best Friend

♥

We can only accept friendship
from others to the degree that we
give it to ourselves.

Kimberly Kirberger

Being a friend to yourself is as important as anything
you will ever do. If you allow yourself to just think about
it, it really does make sense. Once you become aware of
being a friend to yourself, circumstances begin to change
immediately. Once you put it into your head (and heart)
that you want to be a friend to yourself, things will
instantly begin to improve for you. This is a promise.

There are certain things, certain pieces of wisdom,
that you can't hear too many times. Every time you hear
them it is like you think, *Oh yeah!* Being your own best
friend is one of those things. The more you focus on
being a friend to yourself, the better friend you will be to

yourself. And the better friend you are to yourself, the better friend you will be to others. All in all, the end result of being good to yourself is more inner peace, self-esteem and overall happiness.

I have made a list of some things that can help you be a friend to yourself. Much of what is needed to make this work is simply being aware of it as a goal. Think to yourself as often as possible, "What is the best thing to do for myself in this situation?" or "What would I tell my best friend to do?"

- Stand up for yourself, your ideas, or what is right or wrong—even when you are the only one.
- Don't say bad things about yourself to other people or to yourself.
- Spend quality time with yourself.
- Plan something fun to do once a week.
- Focus on your attributes.
- Save money. (Even if it isn't a huge amount, it does something for your sense of security to know you always have a stash of money somewhere.)
- Exercise.
- Eat as healthy as you can, BUT allow yourself to eat some junk food on the weekends.
- Don't spend time with people who are mean-spirited.
- Think of yourself as a friend. No one deserves to be treated with love and respect more than you do. Do whatever it takes to remember that.
- If you are in a situation that doesn't feel good, leave.
- Keep a gratitude journal. Every day write down five

things that you are grateful for. (This *will* change your life.)

- Spend time with people who make you laugh.
- Take yourself lightly.
- Always ask yourself, "What would I want my best friend to do in this situation?"
- Set goals for yourself (start small) and achieve them.

Remember that self-esteem and being your own best friend are not the same as arrogance or selfishness. Being confident does not mean being conceited. It is very easy to tell the difference. You know when you are being selfish, and you know when you are just taking care of *yourself*. You also know when you are being an arrogant jerk, and when you are simply feeling confident. There is a difference.

Taking care of yourself feels good, whereas being selfish does not. The same is true with confidence. A confident person has no need to put others down. In fact, it is the confident, self-assured person who is supportive of others and wants them to succeed.

Picking Up the Pieces

EMILY STARR

I struggled for weeks, desperately trying to be the legs on which our tottering relationship was balancing. But, eventually, everything toppled over and all I could do was just stand there staring, overcome with shock and anguish, yet too exhausted to pick up the pieces. I *could* have blamed it on him. He had betrayed my trust one too many times. He was too lazy and immature. Or I *could* have blamed it on myself. I was too committed and overprotective. But the more I thought about it, the more I realized that our relationship was strangely similar to the game Jenga. Everything started out solid and sturdy, but as the months progressed pieces of the whole were withdrawn until the shaky structure crumbled to the ground in a heap of hurt feelings, angry tears and painful memories.

The day "us" ended haunted my mind for weeks. I *thought* I could read every look on his face, but that day he wore an expression completely unfamiliar to me. I asked him what was wrong, but deep inside, I knew what he was going to say. His eyes pleaded with mine, and I remember slowly taking off the jacket he had lent me earlier that day. I pressed it to my cheek, breathed in the familiar scent and handed it to him while silent tears flooded my eyes. He brushed a tear aside with his finger and walked away without a single word. I remember looking down at my outcast arms that hung in the frozen air, empty and bare without a soul to reach out to. There weren't any strong arms to hold me, and there wasn't a soothing voice to subdue my pain.

Alexander Graham Bell once said, "When one door closes, another opens. But we often look so regretfully on the closed door that we don't see the one that has opened for us." It took me months to avert my eyes from the door that had been slammed in my face. I stood looking through the keyhole at him living his own life—a life that didn't involve me. I banged on the door, I kicked and screamed 'til I was dizzy, but all I could do was stand outside, looking in.

One day I began to realize that in the midst of all my pain, I had neglected everything that was once important to me. I found myself standing there friendless, my family completely shoved away and several months of my youth wasted on a foolish, teenage boy. A wave of relaxation washed over me, and I knew then and there that I was going to be my own person and rely on no one but myself for my happiness. I was going to live my *own* life no matter who decided to slam their door in my face. Relationships are always collapsing, but only the strong can pick up the pieces and rebuild their lives using their experiences as footholds the next time around.

♥

Put Your Needs <u>First</u>

Putting your needs first means being true to yourself and surrounding yourself with people who will also be true to you. Putting your needs first means accepting only appropriate behavior from others and allowing only respectful and caring people into your life. Putting your needs first means understanding that you deserve to be happy, no matter who you are, what you look like, how smart you are, how much money you have or what kind of clothes you wear. And you can only be happy when you pay attention to your deepest feelings and you make a decision to honor your needs.

—COLIN MORTENSEN

Be Good to <u>Yourself</u>

In order to understand the concept of being a friend to yourself, think about how you act with your very best friend and then make a conscious effort to be that way with yourself. Be supportive, understanding, lighthearted and, most important, when you make a mistake, be forgiving.

—KIMBERLY KIRBERGER

I Can Walk on Water

CRYSTAL DAVIS

I can walk on water
And when I want to I can fly
I can sit on sunshine
And watch the world go by
I am the mountains and the sea
I give life with every breath
I hold the world on fingertips
I soar above the rest
I am who I want to be
I hold my dreams within a grasp
I am part of everything
The future and the past
My body is made by the earth
My soul made from the sky
My life is part of nature's gift
I taste the ocean when I cry
I will live forever
As the wind or as the grass
My body may give up
But my soul will surely last

I am eternity
I never fade
I am the stuff
From which you are made
I can walk on water
And if I want to I can fly
I can do whatever
All I have to do is try.

♥

No Guarantees

I learned the hard way that I cannot always count on others to respect my feelings, even if I respect theirs. Being a good person doesn't guarantee that others will be good people, too. You only have control over yourself and how you choose to be as a person. As for others, you can only choose to accept them or walk away.

—COLIN MORTENSEN

♥

Take Care of Yourself

To answer the question of how well you're loving yourself, ask yourself the following question: Do you spend a lot of time focusing on other people's problems? It's much easier to focus on the problems of others than to deal with our own flaws. Maybe we look at other people's problems because we are truly concerned with their well-being. Or maybe we do it because we feel responsible for other people—more responsible, even, than we feel for ourselves. If you develop a good, caring, honest relationship with yourself, you will be able to help others when they need it. When you take good care of yourself and your emotional life, you allow others to see you as a model of self-love. You automatically pass it around. If you want to have a positive influence on your friends or family, do it by setting an example through your own behavior.

—COLIN MORTENSEN

Love Bloomed for Me

NATALIE PITTSFORD

The truth is, love bloomed for me when I learned to love myself. That might sound strange, but it's true. For as long as I can remember, I've been a crowd-pleaser, always doing and being all that was expected of me. Never raise your voice or voice your opinions, sit up straight, smile. It got to the point where that very smile, my ever-present trademark, was all that I had left. I sort of hid behind it, took refuge in it.

Near the end of eighth grade, I started to rapidly change and grow as a person. I must have been afraid that people would not like the flower slowly blooming within me, the person that I'd become. So I practically withdrew from the crowd. The feelings of desperate loneliness, longing and sadness I felt then still sting today. I wanted so much for someone to see how much I suffered, but no one saw. I wanted my cries to be heard, but everyone was too absorbed in their own problems. Most of all, I wanted to be loved. Oh sure, lots of people love me—my family and my friends. But I guess I was looking for someone to truly know and understand *me*, to love me and not leave, to be there for me to lean on when things got bad.

After much heartache, I've finally found that person— the person I want, the person I need. On the way out the door one morning, I glanced in the mirror and was struck with the notion that until I stop relying on other people for my own happiness and self-worth, I will never be happy. It was then that I realized I do not have to hide behind my smile. It's okay to be sad or worried or scared. And it's okay to just break down and cry if I need to. I don't have to be perfect, just true to myself.

Things didn't change overnight for me, but I'm getting there. I'm learning every day that the more I love myself, the more the rest falls into place.

♥

Stand Up for What You Believe In

Ultimately we earn people's respect when we stand up for what we believe in. Being yourself, regardless of the social context, epitomizes strength. Strangely enough, even the people who might feel offended by you "being yourself" will ultimately respect you more than they will people who just agree with them out of fear.

—COLIN MORTENSEN

Enjoying Being Me

JENNA BUTRENCHUK

True beauty is inside, but
true intelligence is knowing it.

Jenna Butrenchuk

I am seventeen years of age. I'm single—in fact, I have always been single. As a student in my final year of high school, I am ashamed to admit that I have never even been kissed.

This used to bother me a lot. The thought of why no boy was attracted to me plagued me endlessly. I hypothesized the reasons: I am short and underweight; I have plain features, freckles and stringy brown hair. I am not the type of person who gets noticed. Sometimes my own friends don't even see me when we pass in the school hallways—even when I am shouting their names.

This bothered me more and more as high school continued. I'd find myself scowling at dating couples and acting awkward around my girlfriends. Did they think I was abnormal because I had been single my entire life? What was wrong with me? This is high school! It's practically a requirement to pair up.

I tried to pay attention in class, but my eyes would wander around the room looking for prospects. I'd form lists in my head of boys I liked, guys who I would settle for and even ones who I would be willing to tolerate for a while to finally have something on my relationship record. At the end of each day, I'd scrawl these names onto my bathroom shower screen and circle the most probable option.

One night, I was really upset. I stood in the shower crying and mumbling. Was I a freak? Is that why no one has ever been interested in me? I lifted my hand and formed every boy's name that had ever been written on that screen. I stared at these names for a long time as the mist from the hot water started to slowly erase them. Before they could all disappear I numbly reached up and wiped them all away. One name replaced them all—mine.

I smiled for the first time in months when I began to understand the word's meaning. I have to love and appreciate myself before I begin to worry about others loving me. Maybe I wasn't ready for someone else in my life yet, and it didn't really matter if I was or not. There is no shame in being single.

As I stepped out of the shower that night, I began thinking about all my good qualities. I smiled again, believing that when I am ready for it someone will notice me. As for the time being, I would just enjoy being me.

Boundaries and Limits

When we are unable to set boundaries and limits, we tend to resent other people who do. If we are always there for a friend, day or night, even if we really don't want to be, we want them to do the same for us. But if they are intent on taking care of themselves, and it is late and they are tired, and they ask, "Can it wait until tomorrow?" our tendency is to think they don't love us like we love them.

The key to avoiding a situation like this is for you to set boundaries as well. We all want to be a good friend and part of that is being there for our friends when they need us. However, we should not take that to an extreme that denies our own needs. Just remember that <u>your</u> needs are important, too. By saying no when you need to, you are being good to yourself and that's okay. By taking care of yourself, you won't get your feelings hurt when a friend chooses to do the same.

—Kimberly Kirberger

Accepting Sadness

Everything in life has its two sides: day and night, young and old, good and bad, and happy and sad. If we did not know sadness, we could not know happiness. Most people, including myself, try to avoid feeling down or depressed. Too often, if we are feeling sad or depressed, we think we have to do whatever it takes to snap out of it. What I have learned, however, is that resisting negative feelings only makes them stronger. Trying to avoid pain only makes it worse. The best thing to do when we get sad is to accept it.* Use it as a time to be by yourself and listen to music or reflect and write in your journal. There are good things about feeling sad and vulnerable. It can be a time filled with insight and answers to questions like:

- What is important to me?
- What does it mean to love yourself?
- What do I need?

You will find that the answers to these questions are very clear to you when you are hurting. It is in these moments that you can learn what it is to love yourself and to be your own best friend.

*If depression lasts longer than one or two weeks and other symptoms are present such as an inability to sleep at night, sleeping a lot during the day, change in appetite, or a feeling of being disconnected, etc., you should tell your parents and possibly see a doctor. At the back of this book you will find some suggested reading about clinical depression as well as hotline numbers you can call. Do not hesitate to reach out for help. As is true with any illness, clinical depression requires the aid of a medical expert.

—KIMBERLY KIRBERGER

Some Thoughts on "Being Your Own Best Friend"

Am I my own best friend? That's a tough question, and if I were to be completely honest, I would have to answer "not really." If someone treated me the way I treat myself, I would not consider that person a very good friend at all. When I think about a question like this, I think of all the times I criticize myself for the way I look or the mistakes I make.

Just writing this makes me want to be gentler on myself. Next time I get mad at myself for something I will ask myself, *Would I say that to my best friend?* Think about it: Do we really treat ourselves like we treat our best friends? Why not?

—ASHLEY NICHOLE PAINTNER

Why am I my own best friend? I am the only one who I can trust 100 percent of the time. I've been through many challenges in my life, which have prohibited me from doing things as well as others. People don't understand that I have problems or maybe they choose not to care. Despite all this, more than anything, I count on myself to pull myself over the obstacles.

I had back surgery when I was ten and foot surgery just last winter. I have trouble moving around, but I am very athletic. I have chosen not to let my "gifts" determine what I can and cannot do. When I can't count on others, I must count on myself.

Sometimes loving yourself is the only thing that will keep you optimistic. When the world turns its back on you, you turn your back on the world and walk alone.

—DAN "RUDY" MULHAUSEN

Three

What Is Friendship?

Be courteous to all, but intimate with few, and let those few be well tried before you give them your confidence. True friendship is a plant of slow growth, and must undergo and withstand the shocks of adversity before it is entitled to the appellation.

George Washington

What Is Friendship?

---♥---

I have learned that to have
a good friend is the purest of all God's
gifts, for it is a love that has no
exchange of payment.

Frances Farmer

Now that we have looked at both being ourselves and
being our own best friend, we are ready to take a close
look at friendship itself—what makes a good friend and
what friendship means to us.

Everyone has a different idea about what makes a
good friend. Yet there are common denominators found
in all of our definitions of friendship. Kindness and support are two qualities in a friend that would be on most
everyone's list. Companionship is another—a friend is
someone to spend time with and to do things with. A
friend is also someone we turn to in times of need and
someone we want to share our successes with. A friend
is someone we laugh with and someone we cry with. A

friend is someone who will be there for us. Sometimes we just want someone to be there and not say a single word or do a single thing. Sometimes we desperately need advice and physical support. The one thing we all need from our friends and by far the most important thing in any friendship is trust. Although I have definitely heard people describe trust differently, everyone agrees there is no friendship without it.

We can find friendship with our family members and with our significant others. Most of our friendships are with people our same age and same sex. There are more friendships between boys and girls these days, and these are important, too. I think it's also important to have friends who are older or younger than us, so that we can broaden our perspectives, learn things we might not have otherwise, and not get stuck in patterns because they are comfortable or safe. It's good to have friends who bring you new and different ways of looking at the world.

In this chapter we look at the different qualities that make a friend. We'll look at what friendship is and how very important this special bond is in all of our lives.

Friendship Lives On

TANNIA MILLEN

I remember the first time I saw her. My future best friend. She came into the room looking nervous and unsure. She was wearing a red hat with a few strands of blond hair hanging at her shoulders. I could tell she was as new to this world as I was. We sat across the room glancing scared looks at each other. Then my name was called, and it was my turn to see the doctor. I hoped it wasn't the last time we would meet.

The next week I went into the hospital for my first round of chemotherapy. She was my roommate. Her hair was completely gone, and she was hiding her hairless head under her red hat. We introduced ourselves. Her name was Lyssa. She was seventeen and was diagnosed with leukemia. She was in for her second round of treatment. We spent the next three weeks getting to know each other and being sick to our stomachs. She was there when I started to lose my hair. We cried together and struggled to be normal teenagers. The treatment was hard, but Lyssa made it much easier. After my three weeks were up, I went home. We exchanged addresses and decided that we would write. We never did. Two weeks later I was back in for more chemo. Lyssa had never left. We passed the time by doing our nails (she always had nice nails) and watching TV.

Mornings were the worst in the cancer ward. The vacuum guy came every morning at 8:00 A.M. Way too early for us. We hated it. Lyssa devised a brilliant plan for us to hide our heads under our pillows, pretend we were sleeping, turn off the lights and hope he would not come into our room with that thing. It worked for a week—our room was disgustingly dirty. We had popcorn fights, gummy bear fights and jelly bean fights. There were medical wrappers on the floor, spilt drinks and food all over. Lyssa and I were very proud that we had been able to make our hospital room look more like home.

For the next six months, we were roommates off and on. Lyssa never left the hospital. Finally the day for Lyssa's last treatment arrived. She had a huge party to celebrate. After being in and out of intensive care and emergency surgery, and experiencing tons of medical scares, she was finally going home. That was the last time I ever saw her truly happy.

It seemed that no time had passed, when suddenly she was back in the hospital again. Her cancer had returned, and she couldn't do any more chemotherapy. There was nothing more that could be done. We cried together over the phone, and I drove up to the hospital. They decided to let her go home.

The following week I was in the hospital for more chemotherapy. The nurses were watching me closely. I guess they thought I might not be myself. It was the first time I had been at the hospital without Lyssa, and I missed her. I missed that glow of hers that seemed to attract people to her. I missed being able to tell her all my hopes, fears, dreams and problems. She made me want to live.

A few weeks later, the good news came. The doctors decided that they would do a new experimental bone marrow transplant on Lyssa. Unfortunately, no one in her family matched Lyssa's bone marrow type, so they went to the marrow bank. Luckily, they found a match. We were very hopeful. She had to be confined to her hospital room for a month following the transplant. I would go and visit her when I could, and each time she seemed to be more and more depressed. Her glow started to fade. I knew she was dying, and I didn't know what to do. I felt helpless. If I knew that rainy Saturday night would be the last time I got to talk to her, I would have said so much more. I would have told her how much she meant to me, how much easier she had made my life and how much I loved her.

My mom had told me that she would be driving past the hospital and would be stopping to visit her. Since I couldn't go, I decided to make a picture for her to hang on the wall and brighten up her room. It was a picture of Winnie the Pooh walking through the forest with all his friends. I colored it and attached to it things that were important to us. I taped chopsticks in memory of Chinese food, hair clips in hopes of our growing lots of hair and pictures of all the friends we had made in the hospital. My mom took it to Lyssa and visited with her for awhile. That night she died. She went peacefully in her sleep while her mom and sister were beside her.

Her funeral was the most difficult thing I have ever gone through. Lyssa's mom told me that just before she died she had read my letter over and over again until she fell asleep. It made me feel good to know that Lyssa had been able to read, at least, how much I loved her and how very important she was to me.

I sometimes feel alone in the world, like I have no one to talk to these days. Every time I get discouraged I remember my best friend, Lyssa, and how she fought until the end. I remember the fun and good times we had together, and it makes me happier. She made me want to be a better person. I know I am not alone even though I can't see her and talk to her face-to-face. I can feel her, and I know she is watching over me. She is my guardian angel. She taught me that friendship is for-ever, and the little things do count.

In memory of Lyssa
December 15, 1981–June 18, 1999

♥

The Shelter of Friendship

It takes a lot for people to push their insecurities aside and allow others to look right into their souls. But the reward for being vulnerable is that deep sense of belonging that only a true friendship can give. My mother once told me about a saying in Spanish that describes friendship: "Mis amigos son las personas con las que me entiendo." Translated it means: "Friendship is a place where I can understand myself with someone else."

We need our friends to help us understand and love ourselves. It also means that friendships should be safe places where our deepest secrets and our most painful weaknesses can find shelter and will never be used against us. I am lucky because I have friendships like this.

—COLIN MORTENSEN

A Friend Is . . .

REBECCA HEYDON*

Where would we be without our friendships? We'd probably still be in that hole that we wanted to crawl into when we felt really bad, but didn't because our friend told us not to. Friends are the most important treasures in the world. Some people think it's sports, or smarts, or money or other materialistic comforts. But they're wrong. They may not know it yet, but they are. What's going to comfort you when your mom dies? What's going to let you cry when you go through your first breakup? Money isn't going to get you through those hard times—friends are.

Friendship is what happens when it's your first day at school and you're afraid to talk to anybody, but then that one person talks to you and all you say in the first few conversations is, "Me, too!" or "I can't believe that happened to you, too!" Friendship is what gets you through all the third-grade boys making fun of you. It's going to each other's houses when you're still in your PJs, and opening up the fridge because you know where the orange juice will be.

*Rebecca Heydon won the "What Is Friendship?" contest we ran on our Web site, www.love4teens.com.

Friendship is staying on the phone talking about nothing or singing songs for hours, and then calling each other right back after dinner to "talk." Friendship is about pushing the humor and rules further than the ordinary person could, but not going too far. It's what makes you happy after being out sick from school all day, because your friend calls right when she gets home—because she's worried about you.

Friendship is not jealousy or envy. It's when you don't long for what your friend has, because you know that whatever she has is yours to share. You support your friends and their talents, and never make fun of them. Friendship is not being in the limelight all the time.

Friendship is what gets you through running miles, endless crunches and push-ups you have to do at practice, because she tells you it'll be worth it when the time comes for the game. And she's right—it is. It's covering for each other at work, because you just had to go to that once-in-a-lifetime concert, or your boyfriend just got back from college and you haven't seen him in two months.

Friendship is studying for finals together, and getting home in time for curfew when the other one doesn't even have one. Friendship is going to see her in her first musical, when you have hours of homework to do. And it's giving up your Sunday to watch her first meet. It's being able to call when you've forgotten your physics lab paper at school and your report is due the next day. Friendship is buying a carnation for your friend because you ended up with the valentine you wanted and she didn't.

Friendship is studying for the SATs together. It's then

calming each other's nerves as you wait to take them. Friendship is what helps you decide which college to go for—the one you've been dreaming of your whole life or the one you can afford. Friendship is opening for your friend that incredibly thin, deathly white envelope that holds the key to her future. Friendship is helping each other pack for college, coming across old albums, and spending four hours crying and laughing over all the memories instead of actually packing.

Friendship is calling each other after the first week of college, because you miss high school and there's this really freaky teacher you have, that you wish she could see. It's getting through the time period where she's never home and never returns your phone calls, either because she's swamped with schoolwork or her answering machine really isn't working. Friendship is taking time out, once school has calmed down a little, just to chat and catch up. It's being able to call, after not talking for months, to cry on her shoulder because you just caught your boyfriend cheating on you.

Friendship lives through wars, diseases, deaths, debts and ordinary bad days. But that's not all it goes through. It goes through birthdays and parties, making the dean's list, making the team, vacations and significant others. Friendship lets you crash and burn when you have to, and always helps you to reach for the stars. It is there when no one else is. Some people think that it is movies, TV, radio or books that bring color to life. But they're wrong. Only friendship can show you the rainbow when it's raining and the sun when everything else is just a blur.

Friendships Are a Journey

Friends are there to defend us, to support us and to challenge us. I value my friends because they have stuck up for me when others have tried to hurt me, and they have bolstered my self-esteem when I was feeling insecure. I especially love my friends because they hold a mirror up to me and make me look at parts of myself that I sometimes don't want to face. That's what a real friend does: helps you see who you are and maybe even helps you to change and become a better person. This kind of intimacy is hard to achieve. It takes a lot of honesty and willingness from both people, and a lot of trust. The quality of a friendship depends entirely on the quality of commitment and the quality of love that two friends develop over a lifetime. Friendships, like life, are a journey, something you struggle for, something that keeps changing and growing, and something that unfolds and takes shape as you live it.

—COLIN MORTENSEN

Friendship

CAROL ELAINE FAIVRE-SCOTT

Each of us has a hidden place
Somewhere deep within ourselves;
A place where we go to get away,
To think things through,
To be alone, to be ourselves.

This unique place, where we confront our deepest
     feelings,
Becomes a storehouse of all our hopes,
All our needs, all our dreams,
And even our unspoken fears.
It encompasses the essence of who we are and what we
     want to be.

But now and then, whether by chance or design,
Someone discovers a way into that place we thought
     was ours alone.
And we allow that person to see, to feel and to share
All the reason, all the uncertainty
And all the emotion we've stored up there.

That person adds new perspective to our hidden realm,
Then quietly settles down in his own corner of our
  special place,
Where a bit of himself will stay forever.

And we call that person a friend.

Sporadic Hugging

MARISA MARCIANO

Marijka and I have known each other since third grade. Not that we've been friends the whole time. We're different. Very different. And it wasn't until fairly recently that we've learned to appreciate those differences.

Acquaintances as the years went by, we were friendly enough in class and greeted each other with "Hi" in the halls. We hung out in completely different crowds. She would be perfecting her cartwheels at lunch, while I would be chatting it up with the boys. We never really paid attention to what the other did. We didn't really care. We were different, so we stayed apart.

Marijka talked about owning a hundred cats and climbing trees and coloring pictures with permanent markers on her favorite jeans. I, on the other hand, thought about pursuing my latest crush and watching what I ate. And my T-shirts seemed to get skimpier by the year.

Eventually, our social groups seemed to orbit closer to one another. We began to talk more in class. I learned that I loved listening to her as she described how much fun it is to run around in bare feet and old clothes in the pouring rain. And for some reason she took an interest in my makeup demonstrations. From these first tentative conversations, our friendship grew. We needed each other. I needed her to show me how great sporadic hugging is. And she needed me to tell her what shade of lipstick looks best on her and how I caught Alex staring at her from across the hall.

When high school began, I was ruthless in my quest to be popular. I started hanging out with the "cool kids" and urged Marijka to do the same. She couldn't be bothered. I thought she was nuts. How could she *not* want to be popular, wear all the latest trends and have lots of boys to choose from? Whenever I talked to her about it, she emphatically told me she just didn't care. I finally started to understand that she meant it; she really didn't need all that stuff to make her happy—and neither did I.

Before I came to know Marijka, I used to look at her and her eccentricities as different and perhaps a little strange. I now look up to her in awe. She is a true free spirit. She longs to grab everything the world has to offer and seal it in a jar. I envy that so much.

In sixteen days, Marijka will be moving to Prince Edward Island, a forty-hour drive from here. I'm terrified. I don't know what I'll do, or what I'll be, without her. I don't know how to spend our last days together or what kind of gift I could give her that could possibly repay her for the thousands of rewards she's bestowed upon me. She has given me confidence, self-worth, patience, independence and a bit of her own free spirit. Lucky for me, I will never be the same.

An Unmistakable Bond

At the core of all of my friendships is an unmistakable bond, but it's still pretty hard to put into words. It is a feeling of knowing I am "at home," in a figurative sense. Being around my friends makes me laugh and smile almost all the time. Even when I am not smiling I feel at ease and peaceful. I know that my friends have seen me at my best and at my worst, and that they still accept and love me. I know that I have sometimes disappointed my friends and that they have disappointed me, and that we have forgiven each other and will always forgive each other. I know that my friends know the real me, and that they help me know myself, and for that I am always grateful (although sometimes the reflection is not as flattering as I'd like it to be). I am unquestionably comfortable with my friends, even in the most uncomfortable situations.

—Colin Mortensen

A Real Friend

JENNIFER "MICKI" DAVISON

All the people that I know
Do not know the real me
For each time I meet someone
I put on a face for them to see
But I have just met someone
Who figured out the truth
And all the things I always feared
Never followed through
He didn't come to hate me
Or see me as a threat
He loved my personality
The moment that we met
He had the same fears as me
And dreams just like I do
And sweetly he confessed to me
He put on a face, too
All the things I dreaded
And all the things I feared
Really are quite common
So, if you feel them, you're not weird.

Closing Open Doors

RACHEL LITTLER

Hugging my knees to my chest, I sat peering out my bedroom window at the autumn leaves falling from the large oak trees outside. I watched the raindrops fall almost as quickly as the tears that streamed down my face. Slowly I moved from my position on the window seat and padded over to my desk. Plopping down, I tucked my feet under me and began rummaging through my drawers. I looked up and caught a glimpse of a picture half hidden by a vase of flowers, and slowly moved it into full view. A tender smile and loving eyes bashfully glowed out at me, a moment frozen in time, one that could never be revisited. Only in my mind did these times of the past still exist. Leaning against the back of my chair, I hung my head, letting the tears fall as the memories of yesterday washed over me. . . .

In a field of wildflowers, giggles and shrieks of laughter could be heard as Grace offered Mr. Kitty a cup of tea. Her pixie face scrunched up in laughter as I offered Baby Bear another cookie at our annual "Teddy Bear Picnic." Grace's golden curls bounced about her petite shoulders while she jumped up, saying "you can't catch me" in her teasing voice. As she ran away, her angelic laughter hung in the air like a lasting promise.

Grace Leianne Johnson was born on April 22, 1984, the same day as me. She has been a part of my life for as long as I can remember. My very first memory, in fact, is of the two of us licking ice cream cones on my front porch while the Idaho sun beat down upon our sun-kissed cheeks. Kathy Johnson, Grace's mom, called us the ragamuffin twins. "Always getting into mischief . . ." she'd tell us. I didn't mind it, though, because, well, it was mostly true. Grace and I were always getting into things and being more of a nuisance than anything else.

We lived a wonderful life, one I wouldn't trade for anything, but even our picture of perfection had its difficulties. Grace came into the world eight weeks premature and weighed a mere two pounds at birth. She was born with one fatal flaw: Her body had not fully developed by the time she was born, and a hole in her heart had been left as an eternal scar. Right before her first open-heart surgery at only five days old, Grace's parents had named her. "Only by the grace of God have you made it this far." Six surgeries and a heart transplant later, Grace was as rambunctious as ever. Little did we know that her heart would not be her greatest downfall.

During the summer before seventh grade, Grace and I were riding our bikes down the dirt path that led to my home when it all began. "Rach, can you stop for a minute?" Grace asked in a voice that still sends chills up my spine. We stopped and sat down in the soft moss that lined the edges of the woods that surrounded our small town. I looked deep into Grace's eyes and was frightened by what I saw. Fear and pain showed through those eyes of eternal happiness and love. Tears welled up in my eyes and my throat went dry as she began the talk that would change my life forever.

"Rach, I went to the doctor today. He said my heart is doing fine. . . ." She choked back tears as I shook my head in impatience.

"What could be so bad? Your heart is fine," I reasoned, but I knew that something was terribly wrong. Grace tilted her head down so I would not see the tears that cascaded down her cheeks, but it was in vain, for she knew I could see more than just her tears; I could see her pain and her fear. I looked at her with pleading eyes as she blurted out, "I have cancer, Rach."

My hand shot up to my mouth as I shook my head in disbelief and the tears threatened to spill over. "No . . ." was all I could utter before I cried out in anguish. I don't know how long we sat there just holding each other, but eternity wouldn't have been enough.

That night I was sitting on my roof outside my bedroom window as I gazed up at the stars that spilled across the sky. I leaned my head against the windowsill and looked up, silently questioning heaven with my tears and cries. I heard a noise and turned my head to see Grace climbing out the window, slowly sitting down next to me, not saying a word. We sat like that for a while, just listening to the cricket's incessant chirping and watching the heavens in wonder. Shooting across the sky was a bright and glorious star, one that I knew would burn out, never to be seen again.

"Make a wish, quick," Grace said quietly.

"I don't believe in wishing on stars anymore," I hoarsely answered. "All the wishing in the world can't stop your cancer," I bitterly added.

Grace looked up at the sky and said, "I still believe. When I was little I used to look up and wish on all the shooting stars. Do you know what I would wish?" I shook my head and bit my lip, trying to stop the tears. "I would wish that we would be friends forever, the kind that can never be replaced."

I looked into her eyes and saw their sincerity, then asked, "What did you wish on this one?"

She looked up at the sky again, the moonlight casting a glow on her soft face. "I wished that we would be friends forever, the kind that can never be replaced," she replied softly. I leaned my head on her shoulder, and she rested her head on mine. We sat there in silence, watching the sky, praying that this moment would never end.

Grace died on October 15, 1996, before her life had even begun. Five days later, she was buried in our small town cemetery. I stood there, in my long black dress, the wind whipping at my soul, trying to be strong, looking, searching for the will to go on. The soothing words of the minister became a fuzzy, unrecognizable sound, faintly droning on in my mind. After the service was over, each person laid a delicate white rose on Grace's casket. I just stood there and watched, unable to move and accept the inevitable. My mother tried to make me leave, but I wriggled out of her grasp. Stepping toward the casket I placed my hand against the smooth wood and touched it lovingly. A solitary tear slid down my face as I laid a delicate bunch of yellow roses on top of the white ones that signified Grace's eternal innocence. "I love you," I whispered, and blew a kiss into the air, hoping, wishing it would reach her in heaven. Turning, I left, leaving behind a part of me, a piece of my soul, a part of who I am forever.

Brushing away the tears, I placed our picture back on my desk. The faint light cast a soft glow about my room, a feeling of warmth and comfort. Slowly I unraveled my feet from under me and pulled myself out of the creaking wicker chair. Wrapping my arms around my body, I traipsed across the room to my open closet door. I reached up on my tiptoes and rummaged through the upper shelf. I started smiling as I slowly lifted down a small oak trunk. Setting it on the carpet beneath my feet, I sat on my knees and opened the lid. Sweet smells drifted from its contents as I closed my eyes, drinking in the moment. I opened them again and looked into my past. Lifting out a small teddy bear, I could hear the laughter ringing in my ears as I hugged it to my chest. My smile broadened as I noticed the well-read letter

Grace had left me for me in her trunk. Settling down, I leaned against the door and read the letter once again.

Dearest Rachel,

I love you. You have been my confidante, my closest friend, my sister . . . my savior. Your honest and simple words have touched my heart and soul like no others' could. You have left a lasting impression on my life, and you have become part of who I am. I know that if you are reading this, God has said it is my time to go, and you are in a lot of pain, pain I will never understand. It hurts so much to know that I can't comfort you when you need it most. Please promise to never forget me, but to let me go. You can't survive if my memory keeps you from moving on. Love me in your heart, but let me go in your mind or your life will never again be full of that happiness and love it used to hold. I will be watching over you from above.

Love always,
Grace Leianne

I sat back and let my last tears fall, staining the well-worn sheets of paper once again. I opened my eyes and swiped at the tears that remained. I placed the letter back in the trunk. Walking over to my desk, I grabbed the picture frame. I trudged back over to the trunk and set it lightly inside. Without another word, I closed the lid of the trunk, locked it and placed it back on its shelf.

With one final look, I closed the closet doors and a chapter in my life.

[Authors' Note: *This is a fictional story with no basis in fact. Persons described herein are also fictional in nature.*]

Audition

JENNY BOKOCH

I always felt like I could talk to you about anything. You know, my whole life, I've never really felt close to any one friend, but I do to you. It's funny, because people were teasing me the other day about how we'll get married when we grow up because we're such good friends. I just smiled, not sure if I really love you romantically or anything, but I *would* love to spend the rest of my life with you because I enjoy your company so much. It's funny, but the things I love about you seem so insignificant, but when you put them all together, they're what make up you. And you're who I really love.

I hadn't wanted to tell anyone that I was trying out for the school play. This was mainly because I was afraid I wouldn't make it, and I really hate having to go back to tell people when I don't succeed. So I kept it all bottled up, and I was so nervous the day of the auditions I thought I would scream. I couldn't stand for it to be quiet that day, because in every moment of silence, I would feel my nerves pound and my pulse race. But auditions came and went, and the next night my mom

brought me to the school to check the callback list when
no one was around.

Honestly I don't remember my heart ever beating
faster than when I was walking up to check that sheet—
except for maybe one time when I made the final round
of a monologue competition. I think the reason some
people hate acting and public speaking is because of
that frightening rush that comes when you're entertaining. But actually, that's exactly what makes me love it so
much. That, and being able to hold people's attention
really excites me. Sometimes I find myself making up
stories, or greatly elaborating them just so people laugh
or listen.

But anyway, as I was walking closer and closer to that
sheet of paper on the door of the theater, I kept thinking
of what I would have to say to people if I didn't make it.
And then, what I'd be able to say to them if I did. I was a
nervous wreck. After one step, I'd be thinking, "There's no
way I'll pull this off" and then after another, "Well, maybe
I at least have a chance," then after another, "Of course I
do." But after that I'd go back to the beginning again. All
this happened over the course of about three minutes,
and when I finally reached the stage door I was afraid to
look. But I gritted my teeth, and I did it. At first, my heart
nearly stopped beating, but then there it was. My very
own name, at the bottom of the second column. I didn't
know whether to be shocked or happy, so I was both, and
I ran back to the van to tell my mom and sister.

That night at home, I didn't want to tell anyone else
just in case it didn't pan out, but I had to tell you. So I

called you, and I just blurted out the entire story about the auditions, and how nervous I was, and how happy I was now. And I was so glad I told you, because unlike other people, you listened. And I can't tell you how comforting that is.

The next day at school, I had this little bubble of happiness around me, and it didn't matter that no one else knew why, because you did. I liked having a little secret to share with you. After class, I saw you walk by so I waved, and you walked up.

"I made this for you," I remember you saying proudly. I opened it, a little card with my name on it. It always made me smile that you were neater and more artistic than I was because, stereotypically, it seemed like it should be the other way around. *Congratulations,* your card said, *on making the callback for* Little Shop of Horrors! It was such a simple, seemingly insignificant thing, but no gift had ever made me happier. I wanted to give you a huge hug and never let go, but instead I just smiled stupidly and thanked you. I was afraid I would cry, to tell you the truth. As dumb as it sounds, it's absolutely true.

Now I understand why parents and grandparents say they'll like whatever you give them as long as it's something from you. Because when you receive a gift from someone you really love, it will be special no matter what it is. And really loving someone is a new feeling for me.

Four

Challenges in Friendship

There is no such thing as an honest friendship that doesn't have as part of it disagreements, hurt feelings, jealousy and anger. The key is to remember that the friendship is the most important thing and your pride, your need to be right, is second. Work it out with your heart and know that the friendship will only get stronger with each challenge.

Kimberly Kirberger

Challenges in Friendship

Life is filled with challenges, and as we get older we come to realize that those challenges are the very things that shape us and make us who we are. It is the same with the challenges that come with friendship.

When we are faced with a challenge, we usually have two choices. We can try to resolve it, or we can decide that the thing presenting the challenge isn't worth the trouble and call it quits. Although there are certainly times where calling it quits is the right thing to do, in most cases all that is needed is commitment and communication.

When we are committed to something it means that no matter how painful or how uncomfortable something is, we will always choose to face it and work it through rather than run away from it. Communication is making a space for discussion and talking about how you feel as opposed to just saying what the other person did wrong. If you can say to a friend, "I got my feelings hurt," rather than, "You hurt my feelings," you are going to be able to resolve the problem much faster.

In dealing with the many challenges that friendship will present to you, try to see them for what they are: small hurdles you need to jump or get through on your way through life. Nothing is so big that it is impossible to get over, and hurt only serves to make us stronger. It is all part of growing up, it happens to everyone, and some day you will look back on all of this and say, "As hard as it was, it made me who I am today. And that is a good thing."

♥

Don't Hide from Your Problems

We all have devastating moments in life, when terrible, even unimaginable things happen that rock our worlds and affect our lives in negative ways. The question is not how to avoid problems, but how to deal with them once they arrive, how to learn from them and how to become stronger because of the tools you gain from the experience. Dealing with life on life's terms—head-on—is not my area of expertise. Most of the time I would rather pretend like my problems don't exist. I tell myself it is easier on my heart that way. But deep down, I know I'm wrong. The only way to begin to heal from a heartbreaking situation is to accept its reality and then become willing to work on healing and changing it.

—Colin Mortensen

So Many Times Before

KATE FLORIG

It wasn't until my freshman year in high school that I truly learned what a best friend is. I'd always wanted someone to go out with every weekend, to talk to on the phone every night and to stand up for me when I wasn't strong enough to do it myself. I had never before had a friend who knew everything about me, but suddenly I had Meghan, who became my best friend from the first day of high school.

We were inseparable; wherever one of us was, the other was probably there, too. We had other friends in common, but the unspoken assumption was that our priority was our time spent together. Weekend plans didn't need to be discussed; we spent them together whether we did something social or just hung out at each other's houses and rented movies. I spent so much time at her house that her mom felt like a second mom to me. Even when Meghan got a boyfriend, that didn't put a wedge between us—he and I became good friends. Whenever I developed a new crush (which was very often), Meghan and her boyfriend would do their best to get any information they could on the unsuspecting guy. I always loved it when I was alone somewhere and people would inevitably ask where Meghan was. It was like I belonged to something; we belonged together.

Then basketball started, the sport that had introduced us to each other in grade school. We both started out on the freshman team, playing junior varsity when needed. After a few games, however, Meghan got moved up to JV full-time. I wouldn't admit it then, but in retrospect I guess I was a little jealous. Our practices were at different times, so we started to see less of each other. And then things started changing. She started spending more time with her boyfriend, and I started hanging out more with my teammates. Phone calls weren't returned, and lunches were spent with other people. Soon we were at the point where weekend plans were cancelled at the last minute, and I was starting to hear that she was talking behind my back. I was at a loss as to what I should do. I couldn't stand the thought of growing apart from my best friend, the one person who knew me better than anyone.

My other friends finally talked me into confronting Meghan and talking about my feelings with her. Unfortunately, that conversation didn't accomplish what I had wanted it to; she ended up deflecting all my concerns with humor and doing her best to make me laugh instead of dealing with the issues at hand. We started to avoid each other at school. The tension was rising.

One Monday night, the time bomb went off. I called Meghan to tell her about my new haircut. As soon as I described it, her voice changed and I could tell something was wrong. The next day at school she wouldn't even look at me. I had no idea why she was so upset. Then one of my friends told me that she had been talking about me in class. She told everyone that I had gotten my hair cut just like she had told me she wanted to get hers cut. Apparently she thought I was trying to look like her, which was the most ridiculous thing I had ever heard since we look nothing alike. So I laughed it off and figured I would give everything a chance to cool down before talking to her.

By the time lunch rolled around, I had heard too much about how mad Meghan was so I decided to confront her. Instead of talking with me, though, she handed me a letter and walked away. I took the letter to a table and read it. I couldn't believe the things she had written. I sat there open-mouthed and teary-eyed as the cruel, hateful words spilled off the paper into my head and my heart. My hands began to tremble, and the paper started to shake. I was so angry, confused and hurt that I barely knew who I was. I couldn't believe that my best friend had deliberately preyed on what she knew were my deepest secrets, fears and insecurities. In the eye of my tornado of emotions, I took out a pen and paper and wrote right back to her. I wrote viciously, trying to prove to myself and to her that I could stand up to her and I was not afraid. I glanced over at her as I wrote. Seeing her laugh casually with her friends as if nothing had even happened spurred me on to write even more bitter words.

Over the next week, we exchanged more and more hurtful notes. We accused and bashed each other, and defended ourselves. We even talked behind each other's backs to our friends. We were ruthless. I was so miserable that entire week that I cried myself to sleep every night. As far as I was concerned, the friendship was over.

That Friday night, my mom was taking me to a party but told me we had to make a few stops first. The next thing I knew, we were at Meghan's house. I told her I wasn't getting out of the car, but when she told me I couldn't go to the party until I had worked things out with Meghan, I dragged myself to the front door. My hands were shaking, and I could feel the tears welling up in my eyes. It was obvious that Meghan's mom was in on the plan because she ushered us in and we all sat down. Our moms looked at each other nervously. I looked at the floor, and I was convinced Meghan was looking at me, gaining satisfaction from watching the tears roll down my cheeks.

Meghan's mom started asking us questions and when neither of us responded, I realized I was going to be that much later to the party so I spoke up. I let everything out. The huge burden I had been carrying on my shoulders for the past week was slowly lifted as we each talked about how we were feeling and what we were going through. It was all out in the open, and suddenly Meghan rose from her seat, crossed the room and with tears in her eyes she put her arms around me in a hug I will never forget.

I'd like to say that we picked right up where we had left off, but in reality our friendship was never quite the

same. We did move on from that night with a new understanding and respect for what it takes to maintain a
friendship. It's been five months since our fight, and just
last weekend we finally were able to go out together. It
makes me happy that we are learning to care about each
other again, but I know that things can't be exactly as
they used to be. Although we do not call ourselves "best
friends" anymore, the loyalty, kindness and understanding that we shared have forever influenced the kind of
friend I want to be. I now know that whenever I am
asked about the friends I have had over the years,
Meghan will be at the top of my list.

♥

Tough Lessons Teach Us

Why is it that we have to go through so much pain to learn lessons? Although I have learned about friendship from good things, I have to admit the big lessons, the ones I still remember, are the ones that came with a price.

I remember the time I got busted telling someone something I had sworn I would never utter to another human being. And it wasn't one of those little things either. My friend had every right to be furious with me—and she was. I suffered so much, and most of the suffering came from knowing I had betrayed my friend's trust. Over time, she forgave me, and I am very grateful for that. But years later, I am also grateful for the lesson it taught me. A secret is now safe with me and it is a very good feeling to know that I have that kind of integrity. However, if you had asked me at the time it was all happening if I would ever be grateful for the experience, I don't think I could have imagined it.

—KIMBERLY KIRBERGER

Be Honest About Your Mistakes

My friend called me a couple nights ago crying hysterically. When she was finally able to speak, she told me she was upset because she had gotten in a fight with a friend and she had delivered a low blow. As bad as she felt about the fight and about the things her friend had said, she felt worse about the fact that she had broken her own code. She had delivered a punch that she knew was below the belt. I reassured her that when her friend was able to hear how terrible she felt about what she had said she would probably forgive her, and luckily she did. If we can be honest about our mistakes instead of being defensive, we stand a much better chance of being forgiven. It is ironic though how often we will take the defensive and try to convince the other person, and ourselves, that we were justified in our wrongdoing. Next time you get in a fight with someone you care about, try to keep the low blows to yourself. Even more important, though, when you do finally talk about it, be willing to admit what you did wrong.

—KIMBERLY KIRBERGER

The Road Is Never Too Long

MEGAN KIMM SNOOK

Time and distance have no meaning.
Being close is an affair of the heart.

Flavia

Lying in front of me on my desk is a silver locket. It is a shining symbol of a special friendship and reminds me of the person I will give it to in a few months' time. Inscribed on the back is a message: "To a friend's house, the road is never too long."

Almost three years ago, I wrote a letter to a girl I'd never seen and thought I'd never meet. I scribbled her address on the envelope and sent it to a small town in Hungary, promptly forgetting about it. I never imagined something so simple would change my life forever and turn it in a different direction.

Edit Sammel won my friendship from the very first letter she sent in reply. She wasn't extravagant or boisterous. Just the opposite: She was shy and thoughtful. I was going through a rough time in my life, and she was just the friend I needed. Later I found out that I wasn't the only lonely one. She needed my friendship, too.

A few months of letter writing turned into a year, then two. The pages grew from a skinny three to a bulky ten. We wrote and wrote. Despite an ocean and thousands of miles between us, we could relate to each other and felt like we were childhood friends. We compared evolution to creation, classical to rock, da Vinci to Monet. She told me about the movies and opera houses in Budapest, while I described the mountains and skyscrapers of the United States. I had discovered a true friend in an amazing way and came to expect a letter in my mailbox with Hungarian stamps every month without fail. I marvel at the great friendship I have gained for the price of a postage stamp.

For the past year I've done every odd job I could find. I've penny-pinched and scrimped. This summer I'll get something priceless in return when I fly halfway across the world and step off the plane in Hungary, meeting Edit face to face for the first time. I know I'll never forget that moment or the hard work it took to get there. We have had many obstacles to bar our rendezvous, like the distance and lack of funds. But we kept hoping and trying to make it work, because the road to a friend's house is never too long or too difficult to travel.

Long-Distance Friendship

One of the most difficult challenges a friendship faces is distance. As much as you intend to call and write, let's face it, it is hard. So much of friendship has to do with the time you spend together and the sharing of similar circumstances like school or camp.

To continue a long-distance friendship, I think trust is the most important element. Know that even though the calls and letters come less and less, the love is still the same. This is proven in that moment you sit down face to face, and it is as if no time has passed at all.

—KIMBERLY KIRBERGER

Through It All

SARAH WALCOTT-SAPP

I know that this world
Isn't always the safest place
I wanted to write this down
Because we could die tomorrow
And you'd never know
Just how much you mean to me
You have always been there
Ready to offer an ear, a hand
Or a shoulder to cry on
The happy times were great
The shared secrets and giggling
The sleepovers and bike rides
The hours spent practicing basketball
And just hanging out
But you pulled me out of the bad times, too
No matter how angry I was
How stupid I acted
How depressed I felt
You and often only you
Stuck by me through everything

(And I do mean everything)
You always seem to know
When to give advice
And when to just listen
Sometimes you are my alter ego
My better half
And sometimes I am yours
I have envied you
And been angry at you
I have stolen your spotlight
And hidden in your shadow
We have bickered
And shared hugs
We have screamed and yelled
And on occasion, cried
But through it all
I have and forever will
Love you as my best friend

One-Sided Friendship

Do you ever feel like you are the only one giving in a friendship? Do you feel like you're the one who calls, you're the one who drives and you're the one always listening, advising and caring? If you find yourself in a one-sided friendship and you are beginning to have feelings of resentment, sometimes just saying something will make a difference. Sometimes people just don't realize they are being selfish and some gentle honesty makes them snap out of it.

There are also cases where if they can't have it "their way" then they aren't interested. If this is the case, then I would say you are better off ending the friendship. There will be a time when you are the one who needs support, and you certainly deserve to have a friend who can give it to you.

—KIMBERLY KIRBERGER

♥

Keep Your Heart Open

Any time we open ourselves up to another person, we become vulnerable and can be hurt easily. Although we might be tempted to close our hearts so as not to feel the pain, it is so much better to stay open and trust that if you do get hurt, you will be able to work it out.

—KIMBERLY KIRBERGER

Suddenly, I Turned Around and My Best Friend Was There

BECKY WELZENBACH

The sky was blue, the sun was bright,
and I didn't need anyone, because I could take on the
   world.
I was ready for anything and everything
   Except
What happened next.
There was something behind me.
Suddenly I turned around.
It was you.
You wanted to make sure I was okay.
You tried to stop me from taking crazy risks.
I didn't need help,
I didn't want a friend.
You were there anyway.

Later on, it was pouring rain.
I needed someone, and I was alone.
I couldn't handle anything
    Before
What happened next.
There was something behind me.
Suddenly I turned around.
It was you.
You were ready with a much-needed hug.
You forgot that I ever abandoned you.
I needed help,
I wanted a friend,
You were there when I needed you.

Whenever the weather changed,
When I was strong and when I fell
I could always count on you.
    Until
What happened next.
There was something behind me.
Suddenly I turned around.
It was you.
You were crying and seemed very alone.
You couldn't make it on your own.
I could give you help.
I could be your friend.
It was my turn to be there for you.

♥

Let Friends Change

Friends are there to let you be yourself and to accept you for who you are now and whoever you may be tomorrow. It's important to remember that people change and grow, and as friends we need to let that happen; we need to lend our support, not our criticism.

—COLIN MORTENSEN

The Rocky Road of Friendship

NATALIE BALTZLEY

I remember the day like it was yesterday. The last day that Sam and I spent in her room. We were in there reading fashion magazines, laughing and talking together like any girls who were best friends and about to start high school together. We were so close and secure in the fact that things would never change. But as so often happens, things changed.

I was more involved in school than Sam was. I was always at a practice or a meeting when she would be home flipping through the channels on television. That is, until she met her friend Grace. Grace opened up new worlds to Sam. Worlds that I had yet to explore. Sam and Grace cruised the mall wearing the skimpiest clothes imaginable, searching for nothing in particular. They only noticed the approving glances of slimy guys, and never the disapproving glances of everyone else.

Our friendship disintegrated until finally I acknowledged

that she was no longer there. There was a dull ache in my heart thinking of how my beloved childhood friend had decided to grow up so quickly and so apart from me. I moved on with my life and successfully completed my freshman year. Sam, who had always been smart, was becoming less successful in the academic field and more successful in the dating field.

I sat with my new friends at lunch but would periodically glance at Sam who now sat with Grace. The two were always surrounded by boys. I was sick with envy at times, because while I could count the number of boyfriends I had had on one hand, Sam would need three pairs of hands.

One sunny day in October at the beginning of our sophomore year, my biology teacher sent me to the bathroom to get water for an experiment. I pushed open the door to the girl's room and was met with heart-wrenching sobs. I stood in front of the sink quietly filling the glass that my teacher had given me and contemplated whether I should leave or attempt to help the miserable girl in the stall. Before I could come up with an answer, the stall door swung open and there stood Sam.

Flashbacks of childhood memories flooded through my mind: swinging on the swing-set in my backyard, playing dress-up in our basements, playing tag with our siblings until dusk when our mothers would have to drag us home, catching lightning bugs and playing in the snow. We had once been so close we could finish each other's sentences, and now we barely spoke. Should I give her a hug and offer sympathy, or should I mumble a hello and get out of here?

I watched the tears roll down her cheeks, leaving tracks in her heavily applied makeup. Her tiny shoulders shook with sobs and I knew I couldn't leave her there in that state.

"Sam, what's wrong?" I whispered to the crying girl before me. As we stood there it felt like no time had passed and we were back in Sam's room reading magazines, laughing and talking.

"Oh, Natalie," she said. "I am so confused. I thought having a boyfriend would be all I needed to be happy. Well, I have a boyfriend and I'm not happy, and I don't know why."

I knew she had boyfriends. Her reputation had preceded her and in her case that wasn't a good thing. It broke my heart to hear the boys talk about why she had all of those boyfriends. Recalling this, I decided to offer my advice.

"Sam, do you want my honest advice?"

She looked up at me, her eyes shining with tears, and silently nodded her head.

"Please give some thought to why you have those boyfriends, and then remember you deserve *real* love." I gave her a hug and took my water back to class.

A few weeks later I was opening my locker when I noticed a white envelope stuck in the vent. I opened it and read the letter inside.

Dear Natalie,

I want to thank you for the advice you gave me in the bathroom the other day. I thought about what you said, and you were right; I was so eager for what I thought was love that I was willing to be treated badly. I never realized that to be loved you have to love yourself first. I also discovered that I stopped respecting myself the day I let Grace replace you in my life. Well, I am taking a break from Grace and boys, and I was wondering if you were free on Friday to get together and hang out.

Love and thanks forever,
Sam

Angels

TAYLOR GRAMPS

A cool breeze floated in through the window of Room 459 causing Maria to shiver. It was cold for November, but she didn't care to shut the window. She didn't dare move, to break the heavy silence that hung between her and her best friend, Tommy. He shifted uncomfortably while she adjusted her white kneesock. Maria was lost inside her own mind and thoughts of what used to be. She was trying so hard to understand what had gone wrong. They had started off the year so close, but ended up so far apart. All she wanted was an explanation of what had gone wrong, and an assurance that they were still close, still best friends.

"What do you want me to say?" asked Tommy, breaking the heavy silence.

"Well . . . I'm not really sure." A lie, of course. She knew exactly what she wanted him to say.

"I can't deny that things have changed, Maria, 'cause they have. We've changed, and we both knew that it would happen eventually." His eyes looked up at her, heavy with sorrow.

"We were so close, Tommy," she told him.

"I know," he replied.

"Doesn't that mean anything? At all? You mean so much to me," she said.

"I know," he repeated.

"I still consider you my best friend," she said.

He looked up at this, and with a half-smile on his face, he uttered, "Good."

"Obviously you don't feel the same," she told him.

He said nothing.

She broke the silence. "I'm just going to give you space . . . that's the only thing I can offer you right now."

"Whatever. I have to go. . . . I have basketball practice." He walked out of the room with long strides, his shoulders sagging in an effort to make his six-foot, three-inch frame shorter.

Maria felt a wet tear slide down her cheek. She didn't care enough to wipe it away. That tear was followed by another, then another. The breeze was still coming through the window, still cooling her legs. She had a pain in her heart so heavy she didn't think it would ever leave. Memories of their friendship floated through her head, one after another, like a river. She gave into them, and just sat thinking. . . .

It was May. The sun was just starting to set, creating a vision of pink skies and purple clouds. It was the perfect night. She was surrounded by her best friends at the

final dance of middle school. A slow song came on—
"Angel of Mine" by Monica. She felt a hand tap her on
the back. She turned around and was looking at Tommy.

"Want to dance?" he asked.

He was her close friend from class. He hated to dance,
so she knew this was a once-in-a-lifetime opportunity.
She nodded, astonished, and followed him out to the
dance floor. She stretched to reach his shoulders, and he
wrapped his arms around her waist tightly. She rested
her head on his chest. He leaned over and began to sing.
The lyrics were so sweet, and he sang them as if each
word were meant only for me.

Maria looked up at him. He smiled at her and began to
speak. "Maria, you mean so much to me. You like . . . inspire
me. You've shown me a person who I want to be, made me
understand what it is to be a good person. You support me
more than anyone. You are truly my angel. I love you."

Maria felt tears well up in her eyes. It was the sweetest thing anyone had ever said to her. "I love you, too,"
she told him and they continued dancing.

"Maria . . . Maria?" Her mind was jarred out of her
fantasy world, and back in Room 459.

"Yeah?" she answered softly.

"Maria . . . are you all right?"

"I'm fine," she told her best friend, Ramona.

"You sure?" Ramona asked.

"No . . . could you walk with me?" Maria asked her shyly.

"Of course," Ramona reassured her. They walked to the gym, where they sat in the bleachers.

"Tommy and I aren't really friends anymore," she finally told Ramona.

"Since when?" Ramona asked, confused.

"Since a few minutes ago, when I told him I was giving him space," she replied, matter-of-factly.

"Well, that's what he needed," Ramona told her.

"I know, I know. But why does it have to hurt so badly? Why is he doing this?"

Maria broke down, and buried her face in Ramona's shoulder.

Ramona sat there in the bleachers, holding her and stroking her hair. "Shhh . . . It'll be okay. Listen, Ria, you aren't the one who's changed. It's him. We've all noticed it. Even me. He thinks he's so great, but really he's just as lost and confused as the rest of us. It will just take longer for him to figure it out. And you know who will be there for him then? You. I know you. And I know Tommy. You guys will be friends again . . . just give it some time and space." She wiped Maria's tear-stained face, and then walked her back to her locker, where Maria hugged her with unending gratitude.

Two years later, Maria spun the combination on her locker. 2 . . . 14 . . . 26. It was the first day of her junior year. Things were going to be different this year. Her boyfriend had graduated last spring, then broke up with her. Some of her older friends were off to college. The halls seemed to buzz with excitement as new freshmen faces found their way around the campus. Her locker sprung open with a thunderous clang, and she was faced with the empty possibilities of a brand-new school year. She closed the locker door, and there was Tommy, all six foot, four inches of him.

"We have to talk," he began.

"We have nothing to talk about, Tommy," Maria told him.

"Yes, we do. We have for a while now," he pressed on.

"Since when do you care about me?" she asked.

"Since eighth grade, at the dance, when I told you that you were my angel," he said.

"I haven't seen that person for two years. He's been gone a long time," she told him.

"No, he hasn't. He's still here. I'm right here," Tommy said.

"Oh, so you were there for me when I was depressed two years ago? You were there for me when my parents got divorced? You were there for me when my boyfriend broke up with me? That's funny, Tommy, I don't seem to remember you being there. In fact, I don't even think you knew about any of it," she said.

"That's because you didn't tell me," he replied.

"You wouldn't have cared. You didn't care about me these past two years, and we both know it. You were too caught up in becoming someone who you weren't. You didn't care who you hurt along the way," she explained.

"Okay, okay, maybe I haven't been the best friend to

you over the years, but don't assume that I didn't care about you," he pleaded.

"Okay, whatever, I have to get to class. We'll talk after school. I have volleyball practice so you have fifteen minutes to talk," she said, bitter towards his sudden change. She turned and walked down the hall, leaving him standing there.

She floated through her classes like a ghost that day. It bothered her that Tommy could just show up and expect to be friends again just like that. She knew that all of his friends had graduated, and he was probably questioning where he belonged. It just didn't seem fair to her that he could come back into her life on his terms.

The final bell rang, and Maria jumped. She suddenly felt nervous. It was time for the "talk." She walked into the gym lobby to find him standing there.

They walked down the hallway together, until they came to a big table and sat down.

"I'm sorry," he said, avoiding eye contact.

"For . . ."

"For everything. I've been sorry for a long time now," he admitted.

"I know. I forgive you," she blurted out. She couldn't believe she said that. She didn't forgive him. She had been hurt too badly. It was then that she heard Ramona's voice: "You guys will be friends again . . . just give it time and space." She had given him time. She had given him space. And it seems they *would* be friends again.

"So, we're cool?" he asked.

"Yeah . . . we're cool," she assured him.

He turned around, and his eyes shone with the same happiness she remembered so well. He wrapped his arms around her tiny frame and kissed her head. She had him back . . . she had her best friend again.

Five

Making Friends

*Somehow within
the mystery of life, we meet.
It is written in
the stars.*

Flavia

Making Friends

My family moved every two years when I was growing up and each time I had to start school (often in the
middle of the year) without the security of a single
friend. At first, I would be too frightened to speak to anyone, so I ate lunch by myself and cried for an hour each
day after school. I wanted my old friends back. I wanted
the security of knowing where I was and who I was with.
I was miserable, and I was certain that I would never be
happy again.

After a week or so, my family would lose patience with
me and I would be sick of having swollen eyes every
morning. I would become determined to make some
friends. It was scary. I would never know if the new people
I talked to were going to embrace me or reject me, but I
knew that making the effort was worth the risk. Nothing
could be worse than what I was going through, not even
rejection.

Each time I made a new friend my confidence grew,
and I began to trust that things would work out okay. I
learned a very important lesson with all of this. Real self-
confidence comes from doing things that we are scared to
do, from taking risks.

When making friends, remember things like love and friendship often have deeper meaning than we can ever know. Some people are meant to be in our lives, and some are not. Trust in this, and do your best not to take a rejection personally. There are many sayings and quotes about the value of friendship. One of the most common themes is that you don't need a lot of friends, just a few good ones. I have found this to be very true.

A Brother's Love

COLIN MORTENSEN

Sometimes we look in all the wrong places and to all the wrong people to get the support we need. It's taken me a while to learn that friendship can be found closer than you think, even in your own home. Growing up, I knew I always had a great friend in my brother. Besides the biological connection we share, there's the common ground and shared history that has kept my brother and me bonded.

My brother and I have an ongoing tradition of never letting the other forget the mishaps that "accidentally" occurred between us during our childhood. To be fair, my "accidents" sometimes involved "accidentally" chasing him around the house with a golf club in my hand, swinging wildly. I preferred the irons (my favorite being the three-iron because you get a fuller swing with a longer club). Although my older brother patented the torturous technique of pinning my arms down with his knees, sitting on my stomach while I was on my back and almost letting his "spittle" drop on my face. If you don't know what spittle is, consider yourself lucky. My favorite memory is the time my brother threw a dart at the dartboard while I happened to be standing in front of it collecting the darts. I remember how he stood there, half-horrified, half-smiling, watching the dart hang from my back, drooping in my bare skin.

He also threw a truck at my knees when I was about four years old. To make matters worse, my dad decided he would make it a Kodak moment. Instead of making sure my brother stopped what he was doing, he pulled out the camera and took a picture. Neither of them feels any shame for this. They framed the picture and it hung in our kitchen for my entire childhood.

Another time that sticks in my mind is both painful and comforting. One night we were staying at my aunt's house and I was really sad about something. I just remember crying and crying in my brother's arms when we were trying to go to bed. I don't even remember what I was so sad about; the important thing is that I have this memory of knowing he was there for me and feeling comforted by him. In looking back, it is nice to know that two brothers could share that kind of emotion with each other without even thinking about it. Society tells guys not to show emotion, especially with each other, but that didn't stop us. We were so innocent. I love that memory.

We had—and still have—a strong bond. Through the years I probably went to my brother too few times when I was having trouble. I wish I had gone to him more often because he has a sweet and caring soul. The times I did confide in him felt very good. My pain or heartache never needed a context or an explanation. That is a feeling I

experience so rarely in my life these days—feeling completely understood without even speaking. More often
than not, my path feels lonely. But I've realized that
discovering my own aloneness is even more of a reason
to cherish a sibling I can relate to and confide in. Sometimes that is all one has, and it can be a most precious
and enduring resource.

Reprinted by permission of Randy Glasbergen.

Put Yourself Out There

Making friends is an essential element to happiness, especially in young adult life where insecurities rule. Understanding the importance of friends is just as important as making them. Remember that you have something unique and wonderful to offer a friend, and let this thought guide you toward the right people. Put yourself out there, surround yourself with good, safe people, and it won't be long until you find yourself exactly where you want to be.

—COLIN MORTENSEN

Bethany's Friendship

MARCO MARROQUIN

Sometimes it seems like
we're all living in some kind of prison.
And the crime is how much we hate
ourselves. . . . When you really look
closely, people are so strange and so
complicated that they're actually
beautiful. Possibly even me.

From the TV show *My So-Called Life*

There are times in a teenager's life when we come face-to-face with disaster. I used to believe that the world was a dark place to live in. I alienated myself from it. I designed a fragile glass window around my soul, so no one could see inside me. Eventually, though, the words of others, as hard as rocks, broke my glass shield into a million pieces that fell at my feet. I was now even more vulnerable to humiliation.

Throughout my childhood, I had to live with people telling me "no" and calling me names like "fatso" or "stupid." Growing up, even in a small town, I had no friends. Nobody would take the time to talk to me and get to know the real me. No one wanted to know how I felt, how much I hurt and how much I needed a friend. I was all alone, still carrying the pieces of my glass shield mixed with the pieces of my slowly breaking heart. I would sit alone everywhere I went, hoping the other kids would not make too much fun of me that day. This routine continued until the last few months of my sophomore year. I prayed every night for a friend. All I wanted was someone to talk with. For a long time, my prayer went unanswered—until I met Bethany.

She saw me sitting alone behind the school one day and invited me to lunch with her and her friends. I accepted, and we have been best friends ever since. Bethany put the pieces of my heart back together, but she didn't fix my broken glass shield. I no longer need the shield because she cares about who I am. She has shown me that the world can be a beautiful place and that I don't need to close myself off from it or hide myself in a shield of glass. We support and listen to each other, and when I need it she defends me from the "hard stones" of others. Bethany's friendship and love have not only fixed my heart, they have made it bigger.

I was a bit of a nerd at school
and was always a little bit different
from the others. All the kids had a
knapsack for their school books
and a lunch box. I had to be different,
so I had a briefcase for my books and
kept my lunch in a paper bag.

AJ of the Backstreet Boys

♥

Making New Friends

Do you have any interests that take you beyond the classroom? Sports or activities such as drama are great places to meet new people. If you go to a church, you may want to check to see if they have a youth group you can join. Many friendships are made through sharing similar hobbies or interests.

—KIMBERLY KIRBERGER

Friendship Is a Bond

BRITTANY KUSSEROW

I stood in the dewy grass, a warm breeze lapping around my ankles and teasing my hair. I stared out into the perfect morning and saw her. I smiled, knowing she was probably waiting impatiently for me to join her for breakfast in the main lodge. I was spending a week at the most amazing place I could think of—church camp.

That's where I met her exactly two years ago. She chose the bunk next to mine in our rickety old cabin, and immediately made an impact on my life. During that week, we had whispered discussions after lights-out, had crazy pillow fights versus all the other girls in our cabin, and formed a strong bond that would never be broken. When the week ended, we vowed to write, but after a few short letters and scribbled notes, we lost touch. I was forlorn, but I knew I'd probably see her next year at camp.

I did. And for the second year in a row, Danielle and I shared a cabin. I couldn't have been happier. As I looked at Danielle standing across the road, I realized something. If you look up "friendship" in the dictionary, you will get a dry, boring, word-for-word definition. But if you look up friendship in your heart, you will learn a very important lesson. Friendship is a bond that is there to help you through the hard times. Friends are the ones who you would do anything for and who would do anything for you. A friend is a person you couldn't stand not knowing. Most importantly, friendship is whatever you make it.

Realizing this, I hurried across the road. I was going to make this friendship everything I could.

We Are Not the Only Ones

We often think that we are the <u>only</u> ones who feel the way we do. We are the only ones who feel insecure. We are the only ones who are scared and lonely when we are in new surroundings. We not only think we are the only ones; we think everyone else is noticing our insecurity or our fear.

We are not the only ones who are feeling anything. We are so similar that it is almost funny when we see how silly we are being to only think of ourselves. If we can remember that everyone is feeling a little shy or a little frightened then we can turn the attention away from ourselves and turn it onto making someone else feel a bit more comfortable. We can say something nice or include someone in a plan so that they will feel better.

It is so helpful to remind ourselves that we are not alone and we are not the focus of other people's attention and judgment. We all want and need the same things. We all simply want to feel accepted.

—KIMBERLY KIRBERGER

Growing Pains

KATHY PETERSON

If your group of friends changes,
it is not a bad thing. It lets you open
up to new friends and experiences
while keeping old ones.

Amber Brockman

When I was younger I often watched the show
Growing Pains. Of course I didn't know what the name
of the show meant, but that didn't matter because Kirk
Cameron was on it and that was the only reason everyone watched it. It wasn't until the arrival of my teenage
years that I understood what the show was about, when
I began to experience some growing pains of my own.

Entering middle school was a big step. I was entering
the age where all my peers tried to be funny, which was
their way of trying to get people to like them and getting
attention. I didn't understand this at first, but soon

enough I joined in with jokes of my own, hoping the "funny stage" would wear off before high school.

Much too quickly the average teenage problems kicked in. My older brothers set out for college, leaving me, the baby of the family, as an only child. I missed them and wanted to talk to them. Seeing that as almost impossible, I turned to my friends.

Well, maybe I shouldn't say "friends." They were more like my clique. All through grade school I had stayed with the same group of four or five girls, who would prove to be the "in" crowd of middle school. We often had fights. I had never really felt that close to them, but we always portrayed our group to the world as "the perfect friends."

Like almost every clique, gossip and rumors about people, even each other, consumed our conversations. We would always talk about members of the clique behind their backs and then pretend to be best friends to their faces. I hate to say it, but I was guilty of this, too.

There would be times, often lasting for months, when the group would pick on one of its own. We delighted in this. As I had often feared, the day came when I was the next victim.

We all sat at the same lunch table. Almost everyone in our grade knew which social group they belonged to according to where they sat at lunch. Mine was the "popular" table, or so the members of the table thought.

Slowly but surely, I saw signs that I wasn't wanted in my clique anymore. They talked about me behind my back and began to completely ignore me.

So I stopped talking at lunch, since almost everything I said gave them something to gossip about on the phone that night. No one wanted to hear what I had to say anyway. Some days it got to the point where I kept silent all through lunch.

I don't know why I didn't find new friends sooner. Maybe it was because I didn't want to leave the "in" crowd, or maybe it was because there was comfort in the familiar. But in the middle of eighth grade I didn't care about being popular anymore, especially in a group where I was unwanted. I finally realized that it was time for me to find some new friends.

I admit that it was hard at first. No one expected me to leave that group. I started to realize that even throughout our childhoods they had never really been true friends. I didn't want to make the same mistake twice. This time I wanted real friends, people I could talk to and be myself around. So the search began.

I couldn't expect any group to take me in and accept me as one of their own just like that. Sure, I knew a lot of people and was friendly with them, but who could I really depend on?

Then I got invited to a new lunch table. Sitting at it was a girl from my church youth group who I had started to get closer with in middle school. I was already acquainted with a few of the other girls. We had several things in common, but I was still a little bit uncomfortable.

It took me a while to feel like I fit in. These girls had known each other for a long time, and I was like a stranger to them. We did things to get to know each other a little better—having parties, going to the movies, etc.—and in time I didn't feel so strange.

Eventually I came to realize that my problems were trivial compared to some of the things other teenagers were going through. My life had been pretty good despite my friendship turmoil: I made good grades, my parents were still married and we got along, and I didn't have any problems with peer pressure. Having to find a new group of supportive friends was a growing pain I was fortunately strong enough to endure.

Choose Your Friends Carefully

High school is a time when many new friend-ships are made. Although it seems like friendships just sort of happen, we want to be somewhat in control of the new friendships we make. If you find yourself with a group of people who are constantly bad-mouthing their "friends" behind their back, keep in mind they will probably do the same to you when you're not around. If you end up in a group that tends to make a huge drama out of every little thing, be sure you are the dramatic type or you could end up more than slightly over-whelmed by it all. Most important, know that if you just have a funny feeling about someone or if you have an actual bad feeling about someone, don't ignore your instincts. Friendships are more important in the teen years than at any other time of your life. Your friends will be there with you through so many important events. It is important to choose them wisely and be sure you both define friendship in the same way.

—KIMBERLY KIRBERGER

Stuff Happens

As we get older values change, people change and, as the saying goes, "stuff happens." The friends you had in grade school or in middle school will not always be the friends you have in high school. Along with the pain of losing friends often comes the feeling of guilt, the feeling that it is your fault that this friendship has ended. Try to remember that growing apart from certain friends is as natural for a teenager as teething is for a toddler. Try to see this as a process and a change rather than as a bad thing.

—KIMBERLY KIRBERGER

Forever Friends

KUNAL BADLANI

As we travel life's long road
We meet and make new friends.
And even though the friends may go
The friendship never ends.

That is how it is with you,
You gave me a fresh start.
You gave me vision, you gave me hope
You touched and healed my heart.

You gave me strength to do the things
You knew that I could do.
You inspired me in so many ways.
I can't begin to repay you.

You're always there when I need you most
Somehow you seem to know.
And that is why I hope and pray
Our friendship continues to grow.

Six

Cliques, Groups and Popularity

_I didn't belong as a kid,
and as a kid, that always bothered
me. If only I'd known that one day
my different-ness would be an
asset, then my early life would
have been much easier._

Bette Midler

Cliques, Groups and Popularity

♥
_____

Just because I wasn't popular or like
the guys who did sports, they didn't
want to know me. I had no real
friends because I was offset from
everybody else. I used to dread going
to school and got upset a lot.

Nick of the Backstreet Boys

_____

Cliques or groups are a very necessary part of teenage
life. Let's face it: Your friends are, at this time, the most
important part of your life. The group that you are part
of is like your home base. You depend on your group of
friends for emotional support, for guidance and for getting to know yourself better. Unfortunately, cliques and
groups can also be the cause of great suffering. Being
excluded or made fun of by a group of peers is horribly
painful, and even though we are aware of the pain it

causes, many of us are guilty of being on the giving end of this behavior as well.

There are no easy answers to surviving the exclusion and cruelty that are part of the social dynamics in high school. Everyone will experience these to some degree, and their experience will more than likely be from both sides of the fence. Although there are complex and interesting explanations for *why* this happens, it does happen and it happens to everyone. Many of you who are reading this may be thinking, *Yeah, right, it doesn't happen to "Miss or Mr. Perfect,"* or, *If it happens to everyone then why am I the one sitting alone at lunch?* Yes, it does happen to different degrees but the point is that it *does* happen to everyone at some time. Everyone suffers at times; everyone feels left out at times; everyone feels unloved at times and everyone is struggling with these same issues. It is part of the growing-up process, much the same as the hormonal changes also taking place.

As for great words of wisdom or advice, here are my top ten suggestions for dealing with cliques, groups and popularity:

10. Remember that everyone is changing during these years, so friendships will change, behaviors will change and you will find yourself caught in the middle at times.

9. You are changing also. Who you are, what you value, and what you like and dislike are all subject to change. This also includes whom you want to spend time with.

8. Because of all this turmoil and the physical changes everyone is going through, people tend to be in bad moods from time to time. You may be the recipient of someone else's bad mood even though there is no justified reason for this.

7. The Golden Rule really comes in handy during the teenage years.

6. The Golden Rule is: "Do unto others as you would have others do unto you." This means trying not to treat other people badly and hoping they will do the same.

5. All the stuff about popularity and cliques will change many times before it's over. You can be the most popular one day and be excluded the next. This applies to everyone.

4. If you are the recipient of another person's cruelty, try your best to understand that it isn't personal.

3. It is perfectly normal to get your feelings hurt when other people do mean and unkind things. Be kind to yourself by not adding to the situation and putting yourself down because you got your feelings hurt.

2. Know that in the end things really do work out for the best. Be grateful for the friends you have and do your best to be a good friend.

1. And the number-one best piece of wisdom: THIS TOO SHALL PASS. *Honest!!*

Popular

CHRISSY FARWELL

Meaningless touches,
Icy stares,
Cold-hearted people,
Millions of glares.
How can they know?
What do they see?
They think that they know,
What goes on inside me.

I can't help but ask,
"Were they once in my shoes?
Have they ever been different?
Have they, too, paid their dues?"
I turn to my parents,
They, too, are dead ends.
They say, "You should grow up,
And find some new friends."

But that's just the problem,
Who wants to be seen,
With someone who's different,
Who's too squeaky clean?

They tell me, "Find people
Who see you for you,
Not the clothes that you wear,
Or the things that you do."

I try to do this,
The next day at school,
But the people I see,
Are too hip or too cool.

Then I realize that,
It's not them, it's me.
I'm putting myself down,
So I cannot see.

That these people here,
With Adidas and Nike,
And flared jeans with platforms,
And hair that is spiky
Are all different, too.

In their own special way.
And I say to myself:
"As of today,
I will see other people,
Not as monsters or geeks,
But will look deep inside them,
And remember we're *all* freaks."

So I walked right up
To the next girl I saw,
Her hair was long

And her skin had no flaws.
I looked at her,
Straight in the eye,
I stuck out my hand,
And I said "Hi!"

Because then I knew,
There was no need to feel shy,
And from then on,
I've been best friends with Li.

So remember my story,
When life seems to get down,
And nobody notices,
A shy little clown.
Just get up your courage,
And go for it, girl!
And always remember
This is also your world.

Staring at Shadows

JENNIFER FOX

She sits by the cafeteria all alone. I want to approach her, but when our eyes meet, she looks away. I look around for someone, maybe a friend of hers she's waiting for, but I have a feeling no one's coming. It seems like her liveliness has faded and her spirit has died, and I grow sad watching her sit all alone.

"Jennifer, what are you doing?" my daze is suddenly interrupted.

I look away. "Hi, Sarah," I murmur as my companion and I disappear into the crowd of careless teenagers.

"She was alone," I mumble.

"Who? Nell? She always is. She's a total freak. She sits there every day by herself. Did you see her shoes? They were green. Who wears green shoes anyway?" Sarah roars.

I cut her off, "Why do you think she's always alone?"

"Who cares," Sarah moans. "Why are you so concerned all of a sudden?"

"I guess I just never really noticed her," I say.

Sarah changes the subject, and then the bell rings.

The day goes by slower than usual and as the time

drags, I can't help but think of her, alone somewhere. I settle my thoughts by telling myself that I will approach her tomorrow, and I even grow excited at the thought of meeting her.

The next day I look for her. She isn't sitting on the wall near the cafeteria like usual, and I wonder where she could be. I keep walking, searching for her gray eyes in the crowd. I approach the cafeteria window.

"Excuse me?" I ask.

The woman in the cafeteria turns. "Yes, dear?"

"Yeah, I was just wondering if you know where Nell is. You know the girl who always sits here."

"Of course," she replies. "She's gone."

My eyes suddenly become question marks.

"She went to live with her mother in Vermont. She didn't fit in here much. She was unhappy and very lonely. I'm sure you knew that. Yesterday was her last day here."

I think about what Sarah had said about her being a freak, and I cringe at her ignorance. "Oh," I say. "I see."

And then I am alone, throbbing with regret. I had probably passed her every day with everybody else and, just like them, was never able to approach her.

I walk over to the nearby wall, the one that Nell sat at yesterday and the day before and the day before that. I look out and onto the crowds of people walking by.

"Hi, Jennifer," some friends say as they walk by. I guess I don't know how she felt; I guess I never will. A tear falls down my cheek, and I wipe it away quickly. I get up from the unfamiliar wall and quickly find my friends.

Tomorrow and every other day I'll pass the wall. And maybe I'll think of her sitting there all alone, and maybe I won't because I never did before. And maybe I'll stop and stare at the shadows of ignorance that continue to flounder without caring that Nell no longer sits there or even that she once did.

Put on the Shoes

RYAN BOVE

Criticism,
Ridicule,
Put-downs,
Rude comments,
Sarcastic remarks,
The joke of every day,
The laughingstock of the grade.
Embarrassed,
Degraded,
Disgraced,
Humiliated,
Mistreated,
Misunderstood,
She is thought of as second-class,
And no good.
A stranger,
A loner,
An outcast,
An outsider,
Left out,

They laugh at her.
They snicker behind her back.
She is defenseless,
Under verbal attack.
Why can't they see,
That she is the same as you and me?
Is it because they misunderstand,
The problem at hand?
How would they feel,
To be left out and mistreated?
How would you feel,
To be laughed at?
Why can't they see her for who she is,
Instead of who she is not?
If they could only put themselves in her shoes,
Then they might stop.

What Goes Around Comes Around

I am aware of the social pressures teens are under and I even understand the need to move on from old friends at times. But I think it is important to at least remember that what goes around comes around. Call it justice, call it karma, call it what you will, but if you are mean and cruel to someone you will pay for it.

If you find yourself in a situation where you need to move on from an old friend, at least do it with kindness. If you are the friend being left behind, know that truer friends will fill the void.

—KIMBERLY KIRBERGER

You Don't Know Me

DANIELLE MORTAG

I know all of your thoughts
and trust me, they are lies.
You can't make assumptions;
You've never looked in my eyes.

There is not an ounce of truth
in any word you say.
Your lips have never spoken to me;
You barely ever look my way.

How can you believe
whatever flows in your ears?
You sure don't know me,
and neither do your peers.

I seriously don't know what you gain
from spreading all these rumors.
You may think it's fun,
but I don't see the humor.

Can you see where I'm coming from?
I really hope you do.
You're trying to gain self-esteem
When people do the same thing to you.

Your vague perception of me
is worthless to my ears.
You have no idea who I am,
so you can't reach my tears.

When Your Friends Don't Like Each Other

For some really strange reason it is very common for one of our dearest friends to despise another one of our dearest friends. As well as being completely confusing **(How could two people I like so much not like each other?)**, it can also be very unsettling. There are the obvious cons, such as trying to make plans and one friend refusing to go if the other is invited. Then there is the emotional agony of feeling in the middle of something that is not at all your doing.

This is a time that calls for standing strong. Refuse to tolerate it. "I am inviting both of you because you are both my friends. The rest is your problem. Work it out or don't, but don't bug me about it." You might want to reassure them first that you love them both and that neither one is going to replace the other. But once you have done that, you have every right to say, "That is all the energy I am giving this thing." My guess is they will come around.

—KIMBERLY KIRBERGER

But When Nighttime Falls

EMILIE TANI

She hides her face
when she's not alone.
She wears a mask,
but it's not her own.

It's everyone else,
she wants to be.
Be just like them,
supposedly free.

Free from the troubles,
the troubles of life.
Free from the sin
and worries and strife.

But when nighttime falls
and she climbs into bed.

Her mask falls apart,
and her heart fills with dread.

She screams and she cries,
but no one can hear.
She wants them to know,
know all of her fear.

Her fear of facing
a world with no mask.
Afraid they won't like her,
afraid they won't ask.

So she waits for the day
with hope in her heart,
When she'll wear her own face,
and make her new start.

The Greatest Gift

AMBER SLOVACEK

My heart was beating at twice its normal rate as I stood in the packed auditorium and listened to the shuffling of bodies and the incessant chatter of the nearly packed house. *How can she do this?* I wondered. My heart was working overtime, and I wasn't even the one about to come out on stage and speak to this crowd. My eyes scanned the room one last time before I took my seat.

As I watched from the front row, my best friend Kerrie walked out from behind the enormous blue curtain and stepped up to the podium. Her voice was clear and confident, but I noticed her hands were shaking as she proceeded to tell her story. As she spoke to the captive audience, my mind drifted back to that night almost one year ago when she went through something that will haunt us both forever.

Kerrie and I had gone through elementary and junior high school as best friends. From the time we could walk, I remember our mothers dressing us alike and taking us to the park or the zoo together. We even looked like sisters, with our slim builds and short dark hair.

But then high school started, and everything seemed to change between us. She wanted to be liked and desperately wanted to fit in. I was more of an individual and did whatever suited me. Kerrie was determined to have the one thing she had always wanted—popularity. And she was willing to do anything to achieve it.

At the end of our freshman year, she finally got what she wanted. She was invited to the biggest party of the year, thrown by the most popular guy in school. There was no stopping Kerrie in her eternal quest for the Holy Grail of popularity. So I put on my best smile and helped her get ready for the party. As I watched her car back out of my driveway, in her biggest smile and my newest dress, I couldn't help but feel a tiny twinge of jealousy that I wasn't invited to the party and that I wouldn't be flirting and dancing with the most popular guys in school. I headed into the house with a big sigh and the tiniest hope in the back of my mind that she wouldn't have a good time, and that she would leave the party and everything could go back to the way it used to be between us.

At about 2:00 A.M., my phone rang. I leaped out of bed assuming it was Kerrie calling to tell me all about the party. Instead the voice on the other end belonged to Kerrie's mother. I could hear the distress in her voice as soon as she spoke.

"I have something to tell you," she blurted out. My heart fell to my knees as I waited for her to tell me more. I knew from the sound of her voice that it was something awful.

"What is it?" I asked, my voice barely above a whisper, though I had no idea why I was whispering.

"Kerrie's been in an accident," she managed between sobs. My mind began racing in shock and terror. "She's fine," her mother managed to say. "But she's in the hospital. She drove home from the party drunk and hit a man in a station wagon. He's going to be fine." After regaining control of my thoughts, I managed to calm and reassure Kerrie's mother and then headed to the hospital to see Kerrie. Over the next few days, I learned more about what had happened. Kerrie told me she had wanted to fit in so badly at the party that she drank whatever anybody gave her. Everybody was drinking, and she wanted to look as cool as they did. She tried to find someone to take her home, because she knew she was not okay to drive, but no one wanted to help her. So she climbed into her car and started to drive home. She lost control and hit the other car while he was waiting at an intersection.

Over the next few weeks, I visited Kerrie every day after school while she was recovering in the hospital. I later attended her hearing. No one who was at the party bothered to come see her or even talk to her. She was a criminal, and they wanted nothing to do with her.

Today, Kerrie gives speeches on the implications of drinking and driving to teens and is active in SADD (Students Against Drunk Driving). I attend as many of her speeches as I can and continue to support her. Kerrie was one of the lucky ones. She survived. Because it was her first offense, she was only required to fulfill community service hours. Teaching others about the dangers of drunk driving motivated Kerrie to continue to tell her story, even after her service hours were completed. On Kerrie's last birthday, I asked her what she wanted and she told me she had already received the greatest gift she could ever receive from me—unconditional love and true friendship.

Just to Be Popular

The biggest mistake you can make is to make friends for all the wrong reasons. Don't befriend people because you want to be in the "in" crowd. Those people will not be lifelong friends. Befriend people because of their positive qualities, because you admire them for who they are and what they do. Look for people who are smart, funny, kind, loving or whatever you consider to be important. I can't stress this enough: <u>Be yourself!</u> While I definitely understand the pressures and heartbreaks of the high school social scene, there's nothing worse than someone who will do anything just to be "popular."

—Colin Mortensen

♥

Be Yourself

I will *never compromise who I am just to be popular. I don't always dress a certain way and act a certain way. I dress like me, which happens to reflect whatever mood I'm in or whatever is clean. I act the way I want to act. I have friends, and I hang out with other people, too. I stand up for what I believe in. A lot of people don't like that, but this world is full of a bunch of followers who strive to be like everyone else. I'm just striving to be myself.*

—LeAnna Lynn Erickson

Look Beyond

The decisions you make as a young adult about who you hang out with will determine who you meet, what you learn, how much you learn and the quality of your experiences. It is important to befriend people who are different from you because they can open doors to new worlds that you wouldn't have even known existed. If you can look beyond the "cliques" and be willing to make new friends, you will get a different perspective on life. You might even learn to see yourself and your "world" in a new light.

—Colin Mortensen

Lead the Way

Why would you want to follow the ideas of others when you can lead the way on your own? Being an individual is what makes a good friend. If your friends hang out with you only because you look, talk and act the same as they do, that's not much of a basis for friendship. The things I cherish about my friends are their quirks or their oddities—that's what makes them special. There is something very comforting in knowing that you don't have to be anybody but yourself with your friends. That kind of support is what friends should provide for you and you for them.

—COLIN MORTENSEN

"Whenever I try to talk to a girl I like,
I turn into a blooming idiot."

Reprinted by permission of Randy Glasbergen.

♥

Friends from Different Groups

My friends got me through the rough times and were there to celebrate the good times with me. We didn't belong to a specific group that could be categorized, like "the jocks" or "the cheerleaders." We came from different groups, we had different interests and talents, and we had different opinions about a lot of things. But the one thing we all agreed upon and the thing that cemented all the relationships was the idea that friendship is one of life's most precious gifts.

—COLIN MORTENSEN

Torrie

TAL VIGDERSON

I wasn't the most popular kid in my high school. In fact, I wasn't popular at all. Actually, I was the kid who everyone loved to hate. You know the one—frequently losing my lunch money to the class bully, even during my junior year, the last one picked for teams. It wasn't fun.

During my sophomore year I drove a car pool for gas money. One of the members was a freshman named Mary. I liked Mary. I think Mary was mildly amused by me. At any rate, she was friendly during our rides home and ignored me the rest of the time. This arrangement was fine by me. You take what you can get.

At the beginning of my junior year, a new girl came to our school. She was from upstate New York. She was very sophisticated. She was tall and beautiful. And best of all, everyone forgot to tell her that she should despise me. As luck would have it, she befriended Mary. And she lived near us. Torrie became the newest member of my car pool. We became instant friends. With Torrie, I found myself not being defensive or trying to pretend to be something else. I could be myself with her, and she liked me. I was confident with Torrie. When I won free tickets to a movie by being the hundred and first caller at four in the morning, Torrie was my "date." When the Rolling Stones came to town and Torrie wanted to ditch school to see them, of course she took me. We became inseparable. The best of friends.

And then it was time for the Junior/Senior Prom. I was terrified to ask anyone out. And yet everyone was going. Even the captain of the chess club. I had to go. And I needed a date. But who could I ask? It never even occurred to me to ask Torrie. She was my "friend." And she was beautiful. Of course, I figured she would be going with some senior or football player.

I finally decided that I had to go and that I had to get up the courage to ask Torrie. It turned out she was hurt that I hadn't asked her before. How ironic life can be sometimes. Torrie, the most beautiful girl in the school, was going to be my date! Even though it was 1980, I decided not to rent the powder-blue tux and instead opted for something a little more understated. When Torrie, dressed in her exquisite East Coast gown unlike the Gunny Sax everyone else was wearing, walked into the banquet hall with me, all eyes were on us. *How did this geek get Torrie?* they were all thinking. I certainly wasn't going to tell them, "We're just friends." I was afraid Torrie might blow my cover. But she didn't. She took my arm and walked in proudly, as if we had been dating for years. It was the finest moment of my then-sixteen years.

My reputation at school changed after that. But Torrie's friendship was the real reward. For years, I had lusted after popularity. And then when I finally had my moment in the sun, I realized that her friendship was the real reward. I had a best friend, and she thought I was cool. That was all that mattered.

Torrie and I stayed friends all through college and for some time afterwards. Then, as people tend to do, we lost touch. I hope to see her again someday because I want to thank her. She taught me a lot about myself and about what is important in life. Popularity is fleeting. I can't even remember the name of our class president. But a true friend stays in your heart forever.

♥

What Kind of Friend Are You?

Since friendships are often by group, it can be almost impossible to have a say about everyone you hang out with. It is up to you to have the courage to speak your heart and mind in an honest way as opposed to just going along with the crowd. You might find yourself in a situation where three of the girls in your group are all mad at "Jamie." You aren't mad at her and have no reason to be. Your challenge will be: Do you speak up and say, "Hey, this is between you guys and Jamie, don't get me involved," do you jump in and try to get everyone to make up, or do you just kind of keep quiet and hope no one says anything to you? It is important to think about these things and even better to think about them before they happen. These very questions are what end up giving you answers about what kind of friend you are and what kind of friends you want.

—KIMBERLY KIRBERGER

All a Matter of Perspective

ERIN STEVENS

Emily

"Marianne has mono," a voice said from across the room.

"Really?" another voice asked.

"Yeah . . ." the first voice continued. "Her doctor thinks it's from a drinking fountain."

"I'm *sure* it's from the fountains," the second voice said sarcastically.

I was impatiently awaiting the return of the graded earth science tests. I had really studied and had my heart set on getting an A.

"Ninety-four," I said aloud, holding my paper up to make sure that the red ink on the page was real. It was (excuse the cliché) as if a huge weight had been lifted from my shoulders.

"Ninety-six," Zoe said, flopping down on a lab stool next to me. "Two problems wrong. Easy ones."

"Good job," I said, my grade seeming less important. *Suck it up, Emily,* I thought to myself. *You did fine. More than fine. Great.*

I glanced across the lab table. Josh was sitting there talking to Mark and Randy. He looked up, and I flashed him a wide smile. He smiled back and nodded his head a little. I felt that if I died right then and there, it would be okay because I would die happy.

Josh called, "Ninety-eight. How about you?"

"Ninety-four," I managed.

"Cool."

I was floating.

Emily was smiling. Just smiling. Every once in a while, she would glance at Josh. I know she likes him. Every time I say so, though, it's, "Zoe, he's *just* my *friend*. If I liked him, I would tell you, okay?"

I know she likes him.

Emily is so pretty and nice and smart. Josh likes her. Mark likes her. Mark told me. He also told me that Josh is only going out with Kelsey to try and make Emily jealous.

Josh is sick.

I was busy being depressed over the fact that I had tried to finish the test too fast and had gotten the last questions wrong when Emily said, "Zoe, I'm so stupid."

"We know," Jenna laughed. I do not know why Emily puts up with her. Jenna would respect her a lot more if Emily would just cave and yell at her.

Emily has such an up-and-down personality. She'll be laughing and then she will start to cry, or be all spacey and then try to be serious. It gets confusing sometimes. And annoying sometimes.

But I'm still sure she likes Josh.

Jenna

Emily and Josh were gazing at each other without either of them knowing that the other person was even looking at them.

How sick.

Josh has problems. Not physically. He has got the most incredible blue eyes and blond hair. Muscular arms and legs. A swimmer's body, really, with broad shoulders. But besides that, he has problems.

He is supposed to like me. Not Emily. But as hard as it is for me to admit, he does like Emily.

She makes me sick. She'll be all, "Jenna, you're so mean!" and everyone feels sorry for her and turns against me. It's pathetic.

Emily is my friend. I just don't know why I get so mad at her sometimes. Oh yeah, I do. Because Josh likes her.

Emily is so perfect it makes me sick. She is really popular. She doesn't think she is, but she is. Not *popular* popular, but everyone wants to be her best friend. Even Josh.

Oh, how I despise that last thought. "Jenna, you're sour, and Emily is sweet," Josh says. Blah, blah, blah. He'll go on, and everyone will agree. I do make fun of Emily and sometimes even Josh, but I can't help it. My mouth runs faster than whatever controls it and my mind can't keep up. But not Emily. She's so pretty, smart, sweet, etc.

Please.

That is *no* reason for Josh to like her, though. Every other guy in the room likes Emily, anyway. She doesn't have to like Josh. I don't have any competition with Kelsey, though. Josh has some twisted idea that going out with her will make Emily like him more.

What a dork.

Mark

Jenna was glaring at Emily. Josh was gazing at Emily. Emily was staring at her test paper.

And I just observe all of this.

Observing is good, though. If you listen and look long enough, you can hear people's thoughts in the expressions on their faces.

The last time I told someone that, she called me a weirdo and walked away.

Emily is so pretty. Green eyes with long lashes, rusty blond hair that curls around her face, a sprinkling of freckles across her nose, at least five foot, seven inches tall. I am continually amazed at how beautiful she really is. Inside and out.

But as the guy-who-likes-her's best friend, I am forbidden to even think about liking her. "You're the only one who knows, Mark. Don't tell anyone," Josh will say. Sure, Mark the perfect buddy whose internal perfect buddy appearance is clouded with the ugly thoughts that are aimed solely at Josh. It's his fault I cannot even like the girl I like. I had to confide that in someone. Or at least let someone else know Josh's big "secret." That is why I had to tell Zoe.

But Josh doesn't have to know I like her. My own thoughts aren't going to tell anyone.

Randy

What a waste. Emily and Josh are in love with each other, and everyone knows it but them. They will never confess their true feelings. Their love will go on unrequited. They will die with unfinished business. Unsaid words.

Yeah, that's happy thinking, Randy, I tell myself.

But it's true.

For me, Zoe is more my type. Gorgeous. Uniquely, yet magnificently gorgeous. She doesn't have the charisma that Emily does, but she has equally as many friends.

She would never like me back. I am at least three inches shorter, obnoxious (as hard as it is for me to admit) and, well, I'm not Zoe's type. She's my type; I'm not hers. Confusing. Oh well . . . I can live with it. For now, at least. But if I'm still like this in tenth grade, I'll have Mark knock some sense into me. He's the only not-lovesick guy I know.

Emily and Josh keep glancing at each other. Unrequited love. What a pity. This would make a great soap opera.

Josh

Smile, Josh, I urged my lips. *A good smile. As nice as Emily's is.*

Emily looked so cute, grinning and giggling with Zoe and Jenna. I like her so much. Kelsey isn't making her jealous. She's too honest and sweet to get jealous. She just avoids me now. At least, as long as I'm around Kelsey.

I told Randy, looking for advice, but he just said, "Gee, I wonder why? Possibly because Kelsey is your *girlfriend?*"

Yeah, he's a lot of help.

Neither is Mark. He changes the subject. Or he goes on about how incredible Emily is. It's like he is trying to fix me up with her. *Hello!* I already like her, man. Mark can be so dense sometimes.

Maybe I should fix him up with Jenna.

Jenna is kind of scary. She may just be evil. Not on the outside, but her fiery brown eyes look as if she wants to destroy Emily. And me.

Emily's green eyes ran into me. They can be so powerful. They send out signals of sweetness and laughter. Not like Jenna's eyes.

"Emily's so pretty, isn't she?" I said quietly to Mark. "What's the answer to number four?" Mark had changed the subject yet again. I'll talk to him about Jenna tomorrow.

Seven

Friends and Lovers

I like you,
You like me.
Should we kiss,
or let it be?

Kimberly Kirberger

Friends and Lovers

Have you ever fallen in love with a friend or had a friend tell you that he or she had "feelings" for you? Have you ever had to let someone down gently by telling them that you would really like to just be friends? How about being on the receiving end of the "I like you as a friend" declaration? Let's face it, when it comes to mixing friendship and romance, things can get pretty confusing and, more often than not, painful.

There are no easy rules or simple advice to give when it comes to the friends-or-lovers dilemma. There *are* ways to simplify and ways to decrease the pain factor, though. Try to be honest with your feelings and do so sooner than later. There will never be a good moment to break your friend's heart or an easy time to admit that you have fallen in love with your longtime buddy. But the sooner you can come clean and get your feelings out in the open, the less time there will be for gossip, rumors and misunderstandings. Be kind with each other's hearts. Remember this is a friend we are dealing with, and if we want the friendship to continue, show respect both to that friend's face and behind his or her back. Last but not least, keep things in perspective.

Remember what is most important (friendship) and what will last the longest (friendship).

Oh, yeah, one more thing. Don't believe it if someone tries to tell you that friendships that turn into relationships don't work. This just isn't so. I married a guy who had been my friend for many years before we started dating. Twelve years later, we are still very happy.

"Is this really your doctor's signature?
I've never heard of someone being
allergic to chick flicks!"

Friends for Life

TINA LEEDS

Tim left for college on a Saturday and I on a Sunday. It would be the first time we had ever been apart over the course of our high school friendship. Ours was more than a normal boy/girl friendship, though. Our close connection was the envy of others. I was in awe of his amazing personality, his hilarious jokes and his little-boy looks. He could read my mind, finish my sentences and bring me to hysterical laughter with only a look. We adored each other. As our last summer together approached, our bond only grew.

The summer started off slowly, with Tim trying to get my mind off the jerk I now refer to as my ex-boyfriend and a total waste of my time. Tim was dating one of my close friends, and had been for a couple of months. I had to sit by and watch as she ridiculed him, made a joke of him in front of our friends, and eventually made him cry when she finally ended it. She broke my best friend's heart, and I ached with him.

We spent hours talking on the phone late at night, comforting each other, giving each other advice and worrying about college. Over the rest of the summer, both of us were single, so we spent all of our time together. Late at night after work, we would meet at cafés and just talk for hours. We grew even closer that summer. I only wondered why our friendship had to get so close now, as we were both preparing to leave for college.

As the time approached when we would have to say good-bye, we went shopping together for school supplies and planned our first rendezvous as college students for a month after we were both at school.

As I left that Saturday morning to take him to school, I was extremely nervous, my stomach full of knots. I kept wondering what was wrong with me during the three-hour car ride. Of course I was going to miss him, but this was not a sad feeling, this was nervousness. As we finished packing him into his tiny room and making it feel like some semblance of home, it hit me—and it hit me hard. I was in love with this guy! And it wasn't the friendship kind of love that I had felt for him through-out high school; it was something much deeper. I felt helpless. I had finally realized my true feelings for my best friend when it was too late. Tears filled my eyes as I sat on his springy, steel bed. I said good-bye to my best friend and the love of my life, wondering if we were really going to meet in a month as planned.

That night at home as I packed my stuff I cried, scared that things would never be the same. We were both going to have our separate lives and would prob-ably barely think of each other. Just then the phone rang, and as I wiped my tears and tried to utter a quiet hello, the voice on the other end let me know everything was going to be okay. It was Tim. Before even saying hello he blurted out, "Tina, we're going to have to make that rendezvous earlier than I thought. How about tonight?"

I was grinning like crazy as I practically hung up on him, jumped in my car without directions and headed for his school. How I got there in such a short time (an hour and forty-five minutes) is irrelevant. What is relevant is that the second I got there, I hugged him and told him I loved him. I had actually done that numerous times before, but this time he pulled away from my embrace, looked into my eyes, told me he loved me, too— and then kissed me. It was a kiss that seemed to contain months, even years, worth of love for each other.

When I left for school the next morning, I had Tim on my mind and in my heart. As I picked up my wallet to get money out to pay for a soda, a tiny piece of paper fell out. It was from Tim and contained words that touch my heart to this day and still make me smile. "Tina, I am so mad at myself for waiting to tell you . . . I love you!" My eyes welled up with tears, and I felt truly happy and at ease with our situation.

I still keep that note from Tim, and we continue to share a remarkable friendship and always will. Only these days we also share much more—three beautiful children and the same last name.

The Smile

LAURIE NUCK

Mama said, "Smile,"
And I tried my very best.
I curved my lips,
And sat up straight,
And held my breath,
Down in my chest.

The camera flashed.
My eyes were closed,
While with a smirk,
And bitter gulp,
I held my awkward pose.

"What is a smile?" I thought.
"Please show me how to make one."
Mama said to smile,
"Someone at least,
Show me how to fake one."
"Liverwurst," he said
To try to make me giggle.

It didn't make me laugh a bit.
I didn't even wiggle.

"Try to think of something funny,"
He said.
I thought and I thought hard,
But nothing seemed funny to me,
Inside of that school yard.

School was tough,
Kids are mean.
"We all have handicaps," they say
But mine was clearly seen.

"Smile," he said,
"Smile big.
Think of Daffy Duck,
Think of Porky Pig."
"You idiot," I thought,
"You're reciting your
Worn-out script.
I wouldn't smile at you
Even if your pants
Got ripped."

School years flew by,
A dozen pictures were taken,
But photographers just aren't good,
With me and smile makin'.
Then one day I met someone.

His dark hair shone,
With summer gold.
The sun lived deep in his heart.
When he first held me,
When we first kissed,
There was that great moment
That the photographer missed.
I smiled a smile, so big,
With such feeling,
That I felt like I flew,
And danced on the ceiling.

The secret to smiling, I feel I found,
Is not being silly and goofing around.
The secret is in loving,
And trusting,
And sharing,
There would be no smiles,
In a world without
Caring.

The Arms of a Friend

NATALIE ABEL

Friends and lovers must be
balanced because when lovers don't
work out, friends will be there
with a shoulder to cry on.

Jenny Sharaf

Sometimes love comes to us unexpectedly and it stays
for a while, bringing much happiness into the lives of
those it touches. Often love will leave a heart just as
quickly as it comes, and it will leave behind much pain
and grief. If asked, God will send a dear friend to comfort the one who has lost love. There is still a void that
may never be completely filled, and hurting may come in
moments not so rare, but the pain won't be quite so hard
to bear in the arms of a friend.

A friend will listen to your sorrows when you cry, and
will rejoice with you when the happy times return by

and by. A friend is one who will stick by you even after being rejected for the mistaken glimpse of love, and will repeatedly listen and comfort you and never ask, "Why?" After much time has gone by and grief does not seem so near, you might find that you have truly fallen in love with the friend so dear.

♥

Choosing Friendship

Last summer my cousin got married. I asked my best guy friend if he would be my "date" to the wedding, and he agreed. When we were dancing, he asked me if I liked him as more than a friend, and wanting to be honest, I told him yes. We danced the night away, and all I could think about was what would happen after this night was over. The August night air was very warm and enveloping, and I thought it was the best moment of my life.

The next day he invited me over to talk. He told me that he did not want to ruin our friendship by becoming involved as more than friends; that he valued my friendship and he did not want to lose it. He then said that he has seen too many people who were friends start going out and eventually lose everything—the relationship and the friendship— when they broke up. He told me he did not want the same for us. I told him that I also valued our friendship too much to risk that.

To this day, we are friends, and I think we will be forever.

—MELISSA AINSWORTH

Christy

ALLIE BUSBY

When a guy stops calling,
chance are he's not worth your time
and effort. Move on and find
someone who actually likes you
and treats you with respect.

Caitlin Owens

We'd been together for almost five months. I thought of him night and day, but I seldom let it show. Although two weeks earlier we had had some painful struggles, I had forgiven him and was trying hard to forget. I loved him more than ever at the moment, the way his hair was so static when it was warm outside, the way my name sounded coming out of his mouth, and more than anything the way he could make me smile without barely even trying. I ran inside, grabbed the phone and dialed Mike's number.

He answered, "Hey."

"Hi," I replied, barely able to control myself.

"Christy, her friend Erica and I went to the movies last night. We saw *The Sixth Sense*," Mike said calmly. Jealousy struck me like a bolt of lightning. I ignored it. "Oh? How was that?"

"Fun."

Something was wrong; we weren't clicking as we usually did. We chatted a little bit more, and eventually the question that had been lingering in my mind for so long was violently slamming around in my body so hard I felt that if I didn't ask, it would eventually kill me. Their phone calls that lasted for hours at a time, his constant talking about her. *Ask it . . . ask it!* "Do you like Christy more than me?"

Silence hung in the air as thick as fog on an early spring morning. "I . . . I don't know."

I saw my heart being torn away from my body and being thrown down on the floor. *I don't know? How could he not know?* After everything we'd been through together, none of that seemed to matter to him now. The constant I love yous, the kisses, the deep stares and the longing I had surely seen in his eyes. He had told me he wanted to marry me someday. This was the boy who had gotten jealous when I had told him of my preschool days and how I had gotten punished for kissing my best friend, Alex, even though Mike and I wouldn't meet for another eight years. There was no way this was the same boy, the same Mike who had been crushed when I told him of my dream to go to a European college. "But

I'd miss you too much," he had protested—and that would have been at least five years away. This could not be the same person. *How could he not—*

"Christy said to call her," Mike said, interrupting my thoughts.

"Now?" I asked, still in shock.

"Yeah."

"Okay . . . bye," I said quietly.

"Bye."

I started to dial Christy's number, even though I didn't want to talk to her. It wasn't that I was mad at her, I just didn't want to hear what I knew she was going to tell me. I hung up the phone halfway through dialing. I felt like I was going to break down and cry. I wanted Mike here. I wanted his arms around me and his soothing voice telling me everything would be all right, that we would get through this. Nevertheless, I knew that would never happen. I had promised almost all of my friends those two weeks before that if he ever did it again we'd be over. *Dignity!* I told myself, *Dignity!*

I picked up the phone again and turned it on, then turned it back off. *How could he do this to me? He's already done it once, and he promised he would never do it again.* He had sounded so sincere that evening. He had whispered sweet nothings to me and had apologized repeatedly. I felt my eyes get fiery, and I watched as my vision returned to that familiar blur. The tears came and, at first, I let them. The silent streams running down my cheeks quickly turned into pitiful sobs as I struggled to gain control of myself and began to choke back my sorrow. Sitting on my cold, hard floor I lied to myself. *Okay, you don't know anything. Maybe nothing happened. You're overreacting, being silly. Call Christy, and she'll tell you nothing happened, everything's fine.* I called and her mother answered, telling me that she was busy and would call me back.

I put the phone down and sat with my knees pulled up tightly to my chest. About to start feeling sorry for myself again, something hit me. For the first time, I felt anger toward him, and I held that anger, kindling it like a fire in my heart. *No!* I screamed inside. *I am not letting myself go through this again.* I picked up the phone once more and dialed his number with skill, having done it so many times before. Nonetheless, as soon as he answered, his voice was like cool rain and it put that fire inside of me out. I was that shy, lonely little girl once more.

"Mike, if you don't know, then we don't belong together," I said so softly that it was practically a whisper. I was on the verge of crying again. *No, stay strong.*

"Yeah . . . all right," he replied.

No! I protested inside. *Fight back! Tell me we can get through this! Say it'll be all right! Mike, please!*

"I'll see ya around then," he said.

"Okay." I slowly hung up the phone.

I did not *just do that. There is no way it's over.* My mind raced back to everything we'd said and done. Now everything seemed unreal. My heart ached at the thought of him; my body yearned for his touch and my lips for his kiss. He was my first love, and at the time, it felt like he would be my last. All of the nights I had been kept awake by provoking thoughts of him, and all the days when the world seemed harsh and frigid, until his eyes rescued mine. All of that was over now as I sat on my floor sobbing away my dreams.

Christy called, and I had been right—he had done it again. Seconds after he had gotten off the phone with me he had called Christy, and when she turned him down he had called Erica. Christy told me about the previous night and how horrible and awkward she had felt while Mike tried to kiss her, the way he had kissed me.

I guess that saying about it takes ten boyfriends to equal one good friend is right after all.

"Boyfriend- or Girlfriend-Lechers"

In high school, I had friends who hit on my girlfriend, which for girls and guys alike is possibly the worst thing that can happen to you. What I still fail to understand is why somebody—your _friend_—would choose to be interested in your girlfriend or boyfriend when there are millions of people to choose from. Why would anyone deliberately set out to betray a friend when the cost is so high to everyone? It could be because these "girlfriend- or boyfriend-lechers" have extremely low self-esteem. These people feel so inferior to their friends that they will do anything to feel that they can "have what we have." The truth is, by going behind somebody's back and flirting with that person's girlfriend or boyfriend, they are proving that they don't have what we have; they _don't_ have respect or integrity.

—COLIN MORTENSEN

To Hide in Fear

REBECCA WOOLF

There were many times I smiled at you,
But I smiled so deep inside
Afraid to show you too much,
All that I had to hide.

A past that had been stripped away
By a tide that washed me dry.
And a past so dark and hesitant,
Never knowing when to cry.

There were nights when I would look at you,
and see me in your eyes.
There were nights when I would cradle truth
forgetting all the lies.

And under all the make-believe,
my smile is all I hide.
And all the truth I keep from you
Is bottled deep inside.

I'm sorry that I've lied to you,
I'm sorry that I'm weak,
I'm sorry that I care for you,
but with words I cannot speak.

I'm ready to start over,
and have you as my friend
And start out fresh and new
to open up to you again.

Just give me time to trust you
And try to comprehend,
That I'm tired of hiding from you
But a heart takes time to mend.

Between the Two of You

If you find out that your best friend is developing feelings for you and the feelings are in no way mutual, the sooner you communicate this the better.

Sometimes having to be the person who does the rejecting is worse than being rejected, especially if the person you have to hurt is your dearest friend. The key is to be gentle, but not so gentle that he or she doesn't get it. If you hear about it before he says anything, it is possible you can spare him some of the humiliation. You can just happen to mention that you are so happy that you don't have to go through the ups and downs of romance with him. "Aren't we lucky to have such a close friendship without having to worry about all the crap that couples have to worry about?" If he brings it up to you, just remember to be kind to his heart. So many things you could say have become a cliché . . . such as, "I don't want to risk losing what we have now." Of course, if that is how you feel then say it anyway. The most reassuring thing you can do for him is to promise to not let his courageous admission hurt the friendship. Even though the first response will be to the "rejection," later he or she will worry about the *friendship as well. If you want to show the ultimate respect, keep it between the two of you. Resist the temptation to tell others. This will only hurt your friend even more.*

However, if the feelings are mutual, then this can be a very happy moment. Don't let your fears ruin it. Yes, it is scary to venture into new territory with someone you have been close with as a friend. But the good news is you already know each other well and you genuinely like each other. There is always a risk of losing the friendship when and if you break up, but if you both agree you aren't going to let that happen, the risk factor decreases. (You may need to take a short break.) One more thing: Be sure to kiss as soon as possible to seal the deal!

—KIMBERLY KIRBERGER

Before

JUSTINE LESCROART

I ran into my past again,
A yesterday to see.

I ran into my memories,
Before I'd known me.

Before you were my best friend,
I didn't have to try.

Before you chanced your loving heart,
I hadn't learned to cry.

Before I learned you loved me,
and I knew I loved you, too.

Before my heart was broken,
which I never thought you'd do.

Before I learned that I could live,
Without you here for me.

Before I moved on from you,
For we'd lost it all, you see.

Before I missed your friendship,
After months of so much more.

Before I learned the worth of it,
When I was hurt and sore.

Before I managed to stay calm,
When I ran into you.

Before I worried afterwards,
Had I done what I should do?

Before tonight I glimpsed there,
What we had before the end.

I hope that we can rebuild that,
For I love you, as a friend.

Once upon a Sometime

JAMIE TUCKER

Sometimes the way you look at me,
Looks like you are in love.
That look, my friend, would tell it all,
'Cept it's not me you're thinking of.

There are times when I make you laugh,
You'll blush or smile or sigh.
And though I know it's her you like,
I can't help but wonder why.

And then there's times I feel so loved,
When in me you do confide.
But it kills me then to hear how good
she makes you feel inside.

Sometimes you're in my daydreams,
And I wish they would come true.
And I wonder if you ever
have those daydreams, too.

And although I search for answers,
On my promise you can depend.
Although what I feel for you is love,
I'll always be your friend.

When Love Enters the Picture

KIMBERLY KIRBERGER

I was talking to some teen friends the other night and we began discussing the difficulties that often arise when one becomes "involved." The difficulties I am referring to are those strange and unusual behaviors that our friends sometimes demonstrate when the friendship goes through changes—for example, when someone gets a boyfriend or girlfriend.

Some examples of what I am talking about include:

- Girls: Your girlfriend has this big attitude whenever you discuss your boyfriend. He was "fine" when you were dreaming of him but now that you are together she only sees his "faults."
- Guys: Your guy friends begin calling you names whenever you are on the phone with your girlfriend.
- Girls: Your best friend starts talking about you behind your back. She says things like, "She is way too available to him," or "She doesn't *really* love him,

she's just doing that drama thing she likes so much."
Or even to your face: "You guys are so sick. Get a
room."
- Guys: Your friends make a federal case out of you
  missing a Friday night card game to be with your
  girlfriend (and call you more names).

Although sad, this is very common behavior. It is easy
to think that the cause of this sudden, cruel behavior is
jealousy. "She is just jealous because I am in love and
she isn't." Or, "I got a beautiful girlfriend and they are
just wishing they had one." Although there is some truth
to these theories, the main cause of their change in
behavior is not due to jealousy, but actually is due to the
fear of CHANGE.

Things are scary enough during the teen years; the
one thing you can rely on and depend on is your friend.
You know he or she will be there for you when you call
late at night. The sleepovers at your girlfriend's house
have been something you count on every Friday night.
Then suddenly the game changes and the phone just
keeps ringing and ringing when you call, or the sleep-
over is canceled because your friend has a date. And
these are just the concrete things that change. There is
also that stupid look that your best friend is wearing,
and your guy friend can't even throw a Frisbee without
running into a tree because his mind is a million miles
away.

If we can remember all this when love enters the picture for us and actually have compassion for our friends,

this scenario can unfold differently. Try to remember that, of course, your friends are happy for you. They just aren't all that happy for themselves. They might feel left out or not part of something that you got to do first. Most likely, they miss you and your friendship and your undivided attention.

Below is a list of suggestions when dealing with "Friends and Lovers." These are not hard, fast rules—just guidelines that can help lead you in the right direction when dealing with these things.

1. Never steal a boyfriend or a girlfriend away from a friend. There are no excuses. NONE.
2. It is best not to get involved with an ex of your friend. There are some exceptions to this, but not many.
3. If you know a friend has a crush on or is interested in someone, leave that person alone for now.
4. Always make time for your friends. Of course you are going to want to spend time with your boyfriend/girlfriend, but don't spend *all* your time with them. Make sure that you have plans with your friends and that you keep them.
5. If you know that your friend's boyfriend or girlfriend got with someone else, tell them. It is never fun to deliver bad news, but it's better to hear it from a friend than from someone else.
6. There are circumstances when your friend will really need you. It is important to show him or her that he or she matters enough to you that you will

cancel plans you have with your boyfriend or girl-friend. If this friend has emergencies all the time, that is a different matter.

7. If possible, spend time together in a group. Everyone likes to feel included, and this can work out great for all.

8. If you have a significant other and your friend does not, try not to talk about your girlfriend/ boyfriend all the time. It gets old real fast and this applies even if you both are involved. Talk about other things.

9. It doesn't hurt to play Cupid every now and then. Of course, it's important to be up-front and honest about playing matchmaker and only do so when both parties are willing.

10. There are cases where no matter what you say or do your friend is just not going to get over your new relationship. In this case all the above guidelines aren't going to make a difference. If you find yourself in a situation where a friend is refusing to come around, back off. See if giving your friend some space will help. If he or she insists on being jealous and unsupportive, I think it's time to call the friendship quits. Think about it. Do you want a friend who doesn't want you to have a love life . . . ever?

♥

Friends Aren't a Part-Time Job

Don't let a girlfriend or a boyfriend get in the way of a friendship. Friends aren't a part-time job; you can't just take six months off because you get into a relationship and then pop back in when you're on your own again. There is a delicate balance that we can strike to enjoy the benefits of all of our relationships.

—COLIN MORTENSEN

No Time

ALLISON ICE

I wrote this poem from personal experience. I would like to tell people not to blow off their friends for anything. When you need them, they might already be gone. I was lucky and my friends forgave me, but some others might not be so fortunate.

My love filled my life,
no time for a single friend.
Every minute devoted to him,
on whom my happiness did depend.

They'd call to talk,
all those friends of mine.
And I'd always say "Sorry,
but I have no time."

I did not care when
my friends slipped away,

'cuz my love made me feel good.
He made everything okay.

He and I lived
in a world we made together.
So happy and carefree,
we'd be in love forever.

Then one day I woke up,
the sun on my face,
and a hint of his shadow.
He was gone without a trace.

I cried and I cried
alone, all by myself.
I could not feel better,
I needed some help.

So I picked up the phone,
called those friends I once had.
They'd help me through this
and be sorry I was sad.

I said, "I need to talk,"
when they got on the line.
But they replied, "I'm sorry,
we just don't have the time."

All I heard was their silence,
as I hung up the phone.
And that's when I realized
that I was all alone.

Watch Out for the Quiet Ones

JOHN PHAM

Love. What can be so fickle as love? What can be so easily gained and so easily lost as love? These questions had not passed through my mind until the summer of 1999. But during that fateful summer, I was stricken with that deadly plague: love.

For convenience sake, we shall call her Carol. I met Carol a summer earlier, courtesy of a summer study program. We hit it off right away and quickly became close friends. When the time was ripe, I asked her to become my girlfriend and she agreed. We tried it out, and to make a long story short, it just didn't work out. For about a year or so, we were off and on, arguing like mad one month and acting like love-crazed zombies the next. This drama lasted quite a while, and when the next summer program was about to begin, it hit its climax. I was with my friend David for the majority of the orientation week. We were talking about the new people in the program, what we did during the school year and girls. David was always the nerdy type, the kind that you could never picture with a girl. Don't get me wrong, he is really a good friend. But him talking about girls? No. With a girl? Never! Time passed by as slowly as a summer's day.

Carol and I once again began getting closer and closer. For the first time in a while, we really shared feelings for each other. These feelings caused us, yet again, to try a relationship. It went smoothly for the first few days or so, but then our dreaded pattern began to rear its ugly head. We started to argue about the dumbest things like whose homework was better or who was smarter. After a few more days, the relationship ended upon mutual agreement. As the weeks went on, we began to patch up our friendship and things were starting to look normal again. In our previous relationships, she always used to ask for another chance with me, so I would think, *Yeah, I'm the man!* I knew she'd be back for more.

That weekend, the whole program was going to take a camping trip. But, before we went, she said she had something to tell me. We sat together on the way there. As she and I were getting comfortable, I felt a strong thumping in my chest. My heart was filled with uncontrollable pride; for the nth time, I had won! Well, what she told me let the air out of that victory. It turned out that the weeks that we had spent apart led her to meet someone else. I was thinking, *Who's the dude? Is he cooler than me? Is he better-looking than me? Smarter than me?* You know, all those airhead questions. Now, you remember my nerdy friend, David, right? The one I said would never get a girl? Well, he got one. Mine! When she finished, it felt like someone had kicked me in the stomach. I just couldn't believe that I had lost her to him. I managed a weak smile and spent the rest of the summer in misery.

This story is not intended for you to learn to watch your back every time you ask someone out. It is more like a reminder to check your head. Watch out for the "pompous meter" in your brain, because being too vain can lose the game for you in the end. Take it from a "not-winner" like me. Keep your eyes open and your ego checked. It just might save your love life.

♥

Should You Tell?

When you think about it, it really isn't that surprising that someone would fall in love with a friend or vice versa. It's just too bad that it can't be a little less complicated and come with a guarantee that, if things don't work out, the friendship will return to its prior status. But all the good things in life come with risks, and loving a friend is certainly no exception.

I wish you the best of luck while exploring friendship and romance, and I believe that if you stay honest and true to yourself you will get through this fairly unscathed. Never be too afraid of the outcome to show your love to another. Love is the one thing that we never run out of, no matter how much of it we give away. In fact, there is a quote that says, "Love isn't love until we give it away." This would be a good one to remember when we are wondering, "Do I tell him/her?"

—KIMBERLY KIRBERGER

What's Mine Is Not Always Yours

One thing I have trouble understanding is when two good friends decide to like the same person. This cannot end in happiness. I know they are thinking, "We don't decide, it just happens." Yes, that is somewhat true, but we definitely have control over whether or not we act on our crushes or feelings of love. If my friend told me she liked Rich, in that moment he would become a nonpossibility for me. And if I told my friend I liked someone, the same better be true for her. No matter how cute he is or how beautiful she is, they are forbidden territory. A NO GO. Leave it alone. Two friends going after the same person is an invitation to a very unhappy place. No one wins.

—KIMBERLY KIRBERGER

Eight

Jealousy, Hurt
and
Betrayal

*Good timber does not
grow with ease. The stronger
the wind, the stronger
the trees.*

J. Willard Marriott

Jealousy, Hurt and Betrayal

"Jenna, why don't you hang out with Lisa anymore?" asked a friend.

"Would you hang out with someone who flirts with your boyfriend whenever she gets a chance? Someone who copies everything you do—your clothes, your hairstyle, even the way you laugh?" Jenna asked.

"I guess not," admitted the friend.

"Would you want to hang out with someone for whom, no matter what you did for her, it was never enough? Would you want to hang out with someone who talks behind your back?" Jenna continued.

"No way," the friend agreed.

"Neither did Lisa," replied Jenna.

No one *wants* to be the recipient of someone else's cruel and selfish behavior. And to be honest, I don't think people enjoy feeling jealous or betraying another person. Yet no one escapes being the target of these emotions and behaviors.

The good news is: The more you understand what is at the heart of the matter, the better you will be able to endure it.

The best way to begin to understand human behavior is to pay attention to yourself and your actions as much as possible. To better understand why a friend you trusted would talk about you behind your back, pay attention to yourself when you do the same thing. Is it intended to hurt the other person, or do you just want to be part of a conversation and this is a way that you can join in? Do you flirt with your friend's boyfriend to hurt her, or is it because you want him to think you are cool? Do you go after a friend's ex to make her jealous, or is it because you think so highly of her that anybody she liked is certainly good enough for you?

The more you are able to examine your own behavior and be honest with yourself about what is behind that behavior, the more you will be able to see that most of what goes on around you has very little to do with you personally.

In this chapter we will look at situations of betrayal and explore the green-eyed monster: jealousy. I hope that I can help you to see things in a more openhearted way, and to establish boundaries that clearly define what you will and will not accept in your friendships.

Also, since you are well on your way to being an adult, you probably already know: All of your actions affect others. We do not live in a bubble where we can simply do what we want, when we want, just because we want, without affecting those around us—most importantly, those we love and care about. This chapter will help you to see both sides of jealousy and betrayal. It will also help you to have more compassion and understanding for yourself as well as others.

♥

Keep Your Friends Accountable

It's important to confront friends who deceive you or betray you. If your friend is willing to admit his or her faults and work on them, your friendship can grow stronger. Keep your friends accountable and let them know that you respect them and that you expect respect in return.

—COLIN MORTENSEN

There All Along

KIMBERLY ANGELIS

I had been friends with Julie since fourth grade. Back then, we spent every weekend at each other's house and traded notes every day at school. We were by anyone's standards the best of friends. Then high school started and everything changed.

The first day of school is difficult and scary for anyone, but it was even more so for me. I had gone to a private middle school and was now switching to the local public high school. Julie and I had talked about it many times on the phone. She knew all the kids from middle school, so she had trouble fully understanding why I was so afraid. She reassured me that she would introduce me to all her friends. Plus, she would always say, we have each other; we don't need anyone else.

I hadn't seen her all day, and when the bell rang for lunch I was a bit freaked. The day had gotten off to a bad start and I felt so out of place. Everyone looked like they knew where they were going and like they had done this a thousand times before. I was frantically looking everywhere for Julie and because of that I proceeded to bump into about twenty people.

That wasn't so bad until I did it with a tray of food. I was trying to get the noodles off my skirt when I finally spotted her. I was so relieved that I shouted her name kind of loudly and headed toward her like she was holding the key to my next breath of air. That was the minute my whole world came tumbling down. She basically acted like she didn't know me. As I got closer to her I noticed she was sitting with a group of kids that she had always talked about as being popular. She looked at me with this kind of blank stare and said, "Sorry, but there isn't any more room here." With that I just burst into tears and ran for the bathroom.

I kept thinking she would call me that night and beg for my forgiveness, but that didn't happen. In fact, when I finally got up the nerve to call her she said she didn't know what to say but she had just outgrown our friendship and me. She explained to me, as if she thought I would say, "Oh, now I understand," that she had matured faster than me and I shouldn't feel bad; I should just try to find friends who were more like me. I hung up the phone and sat there for what seemed like an hour. I had no one to call and no one to cry to because *she* was the one who I had always turned to when I felt like this.

The next day I begged my mom to let me stay home from school, but since I hadn't even bothered to fake an illness she gave me the big talk about being brave and that things will get better and everyone has a hard time their first few days at a new school. I couldn't bring myself to tell her what had happened because some part of me wanted to believe it was a horrible mistake that would right itself as soon as I saw Julie. If my mom hated her, how would I get to spend the weekend at her house eating ice cream and watching old movies?

I was miserable for the first three weeks of high school. Fortunately, I met some great new friends and was becoming more and more at home in my new school. Julie came to school with more makeup and shorter skirts every day, and rarely smiled anymore.

When I finally stopped crying, I tried to hate her. I fantasized about different revenge plots, each one more elaborate than the last. Then, almost as if I had planned it, my chance to get even was laid out right before me.

Julie came to school a total mess. Her hair wasn't combed and you could tell she hadn't slept and her eyes were swollen from hours of crying. As I watched her telling her friends what was wrong I saw their faces change. It was as if a curtain dropped over them and all expression was gone. Julie was getting almost hysterical trying to make them understand how much pain she was in, but the harder she tried the less responsive they were. Have you ever felt someone else's pain in such a strong way that for a minute you forgot it was theirs and not yours? My heart was twisting and I felt her humiliation. One by one they started making excuses to leave, looking at their watches and announcing with faked urgency that they were late for this or that. Julie stood there in shock. Later, she told me that one of the girls in her group had started a nasty rumor about her. She had told everyone horrible things that Julie had supposedly said about them behind their backs. It had spread like wildfire. She had encountered stares and whispers everywhere she went and even her best friends didn't believe her when she said it wasn't true.

There was a voice in my head that was saying, *Time for revenge; go for it:* "Great friends, Julie!" or, "Gee, now I can see why you were willing to throw our friendship away. Why didn't you just tell me what trusting and loyal people they were?"

But almost as soon as I had the thought I had the realization that I no longer wanted or, for that matter, needed revenge. I actually felt bad for her. There was a fear that I was being a sucker, a fool and she would only hurt me again—but none of that mattered in that moment.

I walked up to her slowly, not wanting to frighten her. She was very fragile. I looked at her and she burst into tears. I put my backpack on the ground and pulled her into my arms. She was sobbing now, that kind of crying where your whole body is shaking. I told her I wasn't going anywhere; I would be there for her.

That is when I realized I had been there all along.

It Isn't About You

The preceding story has a happy ending but often this is not the way things go.

Particularly in high school, kids can be heartless and friendships that were once precious can turn into nightmares. As I have said many times before (but it can't be said too much), <u>rarely</u> are these things personal. People who are cruel and heartless to you are generally people who are cruel and heartless.

It is almost impossible—no, it <u>is</u> impossible—to not be hurt by the cruelty of others. But do try to remember that this isn't about you. Call a true friend and let them give you the support and love you need.

—KIMBERLY KIRBERGER

Forgiveness Is a Good Thing

When a friend has betrayed us and hurt us deeply it is difficult to even think about forgiving him or her. What if I forgive my friend and he or she does the same thing to me again? I don't want to be a sucker and give people the message that they can walk all over me and that all they have to do is say they are sorry. There are times when moving on is the right thing to do. Certain betrayals are unforgivable, and you have to decide where you draw the line. But if you find yourself wanting to forgive and forget, by all means go for it and don't worry about being a sucker. The ability to forgive makes you the opposite of a sucker; it makes you a good friend.

—KIMBERLY KIRBERGER

Bad-Mouthing

I don't think it ever gets easy to know people are bad-mouthing you behind your back and not get upset and hurt, especially when it is your "friends" who are doing it. When it happens to me, I literally feel sick and I really get caught up in how unfair it is. The thing that helped me the most with this was a saying, "It is none of my business what other people think about me," and, of course, the same is true for what other people say about me. We cannot control how others feel about us, although we have all tried. People's responses to us are based on many things, some of which have absolutely nothing to do with us.

—KIMBERLY KIRBERGER

Holding On to the Gold

CARRIE SUE O'MALEY

Make new friends
But keep the old
One is silver
And the other gold.

I sang this song over and over during my Girl Scout days. Back then, a "friend" was merely someone with whom I played on the playground and whispered about the boys in class. They came and went, and I never really took a minute to think about their significance, much less decide if they were of gold or silver quality.

As time moved on, however, I began opening up more with my peers. I shared more than my Barbies, My Little Ponies and Care Bears; I shared my soul. I allowed others to look inside me and see more than the shy, giggly exterior. I learned to appreciate others' triumphs with as much pride as my own. I learned that friends are indeed life's greatest gift.

When high school started, I met my best friend. Becky and I had more in common than both being on the swim team. I discovered we shared the same quirky sense of humor, and she appreciated the beauty of animals and sappy love songs as much as I did. A lifelong friendship was cemented. We quickly became inseparable, and we shared everything, from our lockers to our souls.

I cried when she learned of her aunt's cancer. She cried when my first love stomped on my heart. And when high school ended, we both cried because we would be attending separate colleges in the fall.

The first semester of university life was hard on us both. Our phone bills were astronomical, our e-mails ridiculously long. Not an hour went by that I didn't think of her at her school and what she might be doing. When I cried over my first college broken heart, I longed for her to be there. And when I felt out of place and insecure with where my life was going, I needed her to hug me and remind me that everything always works out for the best.

It wasn't until second semester of freshman year that I found friends with whom I felt completely comfortable. These were friends with whom I could be myself, joke around and pour out my feelings. The loneliness that had plagued my heart the semester before was quickly fading away. I was eager to share these great new friends with Becky and Becky with them.

When Becky was finally able to visit me at my school, something unexpected happened. The sparkle in her eyes faded immediately. The heartiness in her laughter ceased. When I introduced her to my new best friends, her eyes grew dark and I could see the hurt within them. My new friends tried to reach out to her and share their friendship, but Becky seemed unwilling to accept it. I was crushed; I didn't understand how the people I loved most couldn't love each other. I found it impossible to understand how she was unable to see the love on my new friends' faces.

Becky left, and I thought long and hard about what had happened when she first arrived at my school. After many unanswered questions, I reluctantly understood that she was jealous. She saw me with my new friends and regretted that we no longer shared the same experiences since we now lived in two different locations. She saw all the fun I was having without her and wished she could be a part of it. She was jealous that these new friends were becoming as big a part of my life as she was. She wished she could be in their position, with me for every triumph and every downfall I encountered in college.

When I think of my friends, they seem to fall into two distinct groups: those from home and those from school. My friends at school all know each other, and we share our own inside jokes; my friends at home all know each other, and we have our own fun. It's almost like two different worlds, and when the two worlds collide, disaster strikes.

I think Becky and I both learned an important lesson from her first visit to my college. We'd always have the friendship that had given us so much happiness through the years. Nothing could ever change the bond we'd

found and the experiences we'd shared. We are both moving in different directions, walking on two different paths
of life. However, through everything, we'll always have
each other. Although she may not be able to hug me
when I cry, she'll still cry because I'm hurting. And
although I won't be able to see her crying, I'll feel her
hurt when she falls down. True friendship stands
through everything.

While new friends are special and exciting, old friends
are always there, waiting to share their heart and soul,
no matter how far apart. Perhaps it is most important
not to forget those who have stood by you through it all,
those who have become gold friends. Becky will always
be my golden best friend.

Foolish Girl

REBECCA WOOLF

I don't know if you know her,
When you say you don't you lie,
And I don't know if you trust her
Or if she's ever made you cry.
And I don't care if you hear me
Or if you turn and walk away,
And I don't care if you talk back
Or have nothing left to say.
'Cause I see you walk on by
With your nose stuck in the air
I watch you roll your eyes
And run your fingers through your hair.
I don't care if you smile at me
'Cause it's plastic anyway,
And I wonder if I touched it
If it would slowly melt away.
Oh, I know that you must know her
And deny the fact she's you,
What a stupid little foolish girl
That I can see right through.

♥

Wrong Place, Wrong Time

Ninety-nine percent of the time when someone is cruel or mean to you it is because they have been hurt and want to hurt back. Oftentimes the person who hurt them was not you but someone they can't do battle with head-on. You aren't the person who hurt them, you are just in the wrong place at the wrong time.

—KIMBERLY KIRBERGER

You Win

JENNIFER CARDEN

I give,
You take.
I'm real,
You're fake.
I love,
You don't.
I commit,
You won't.
I need,
You don't give in.
I lose,
You win
. . . Again.

"Your mother and I were getting pretty tired of
your bad attitude. That's much better!"

Reprinted by permission of Randy Glasbergen.

Two of a Kind

ROGER TODARO

A lot of guys made fun of me
and gave me a hard time. They would
say, "What's your problem?
Why don't you play basketball
like a normal guy?"

AJ of the Backstreet Boys

We were the best of friends. Inseparable. Everything we did, we did together. You would think we were connected at the hip or something. Then we met her. She was every teen's dream. Like an angel from the midst of God's palace. An angel who could destroy a perfect friendship. An angel who did just that.

It was a new school. Bigger and better than my last school. It was exciting and very scary at the same time. I was amazed at how many people there were, and I wondered how I could ever make friends in a place like this.

I'd never heard the word "stereotype" before. I had just floated around between different peer groups as if I belonged. But it didn't work that way in high school. You couldn't just float around. You had to be chosen. And since I never really had a specific crowd that I belonged to, I didn't get chosen by *any* group. Of course, I had friends who were in all the different circles, but when it came around to hanging out after school and doing things that kids do, I didn't belong. I ended up floating around for the first half a year or so, and then something wonderful happened (or so I thought at the time). I finally got selected by a group. I knew that this wasn't the most popular group of the school, but I was just glad to be accepted.

My grades started dropping, and my regular habits changed dramatically. I was turning into a trouble-maker. I realized that this wasn't what I wanted. Even after being accepted, I didn't like who I had become. I really wanted to get out, and I tried, but none of my other friends would talk to me for fear of their friends ridiculing them. I had nowhere to turn. I could do nothing but be alone or be a "thug."

I chose to be alone.

Sophomore year rolled around, and new faces joined our school. It didn't excite me as much as it used to. Then one day as I was skipping school (which I was doing a lot), I met someone who was in the same predicament I was in. I had never seen him around before, but somehow I knew that Shawn and I would be the greatest of friends. He was an outcast and so was I.

Over the next year or so, Shawn and I started to spend time together. We wouldn't do anything unless the other was there. We spent the night at each other's house, went to the movies, cruised the town, ate burgers at the local Burger King and went looking for girls. I was surprised at the way Shawn had the same tastes and interests as I did. We never argued about anything. We always wanted to see the same movie, order the same pizza, and, unfortunately, go out with the same girl.

It was never a problem before. If I liked someone, he respected that and never went after her. Even after we broke up. That was until *she* came around. (And to emphasize how stupid the whole thing was in the end, I don't even recall her name.)

I was so shy that I never thought I would have a chance with her. I mean, why would she ever take an interest in an outcast like me? I never had the courage to just approach her and start a conversation, much less ask her on a date. I was terrified that she would end up crushing my heart like a cigarette butt under her heel.

But to my surprise, she *did* notice me. One of her friends approached me and told me that the girl of my dreams was interested in *me* and wanted to know what I thought about her. Could this actually be happening to me? I had no clue what to say. After about a minute or so of babbling like an idiot, I told her friend (not in so many words) that I was definitely interested. We exchanged the usual information, and she left to share the news. I didn't know what to do next. Should I wait for her to call me, or should I call her? What would I say to her when we did talk? It was never this complicated before. But it was never an angel before, either.

Shawn was happy for me, or at least acted like he was. He was always spending time with us and would be okay with breaking his plans to do so. I just thought it was great that I could spend time with both my best friend and girlfriend, and not have a problem finding time for them both.

The great times that I shared with Shawn and my girlfriend lasted for about a month. Then, out of the blue, she dropped me like a bad habit. I wouldn't tell any of my friends this, but I bawled like a baby when we broke up. I thought that my life was over, and that I could never go on. But Shawn was there for me, like always, with words of wisdom (at least as much wisdom as we had at sixteen), to help cheer me up and get me back on my feet. "You'll find someone better," or "She wasn't meant for you anyway." It took me a little while, but I finally started to get back on track and move on. But the feelings for her were still there.

Shawn and I acted like things never changed and just started doing the things we used to again.

Then a day I never would've dreamed could happen, happened. I was informed by another friend of mine that Shawn and my ex-girlfriend were getting a little "friendly" with each other. I didn't believe it. Shawn was my best friend, and he would never do that to me. Besides, the source I got the information from wasn't a very reliable one. So, I did what any regular Joe would do in that situation. I asked Shawn.

Never before had I ever wished for someone to lie to me, but I sure wish Shawn would have that day. Instead, he told the truth. It hurt worse than any physical pain I'd ever felt. It felt like he ripped out my heart. I was so angry that all I saw was red. I couldn't think straight because I was filled with so much rage. At the time, I thought it was the worst thing he could ever do to me, and I didn't care about anything he had to say.

We got into our first fight. It wasn't a physical fight, but something a whole lot worse. We yelled and screamed at each other for a couple of hours before I just got fed up and left. And later that night, my world ended. . . .

I heard the phone next to my bed ring, and I was quick to answer it. For some strange reason, I knew it would be him. But I wasn't expecting what I got. I listened to him talk and knew that something wasn't right. I heard a girl laughing and that sound made the blood pound in my ears. The call was quick, but the message lasted forever. To this day, I can still hear those words echoing in my head. "Roger, don't ever talk to me again. I don't want to be your friend anymore. We've never met."

I don't know how long I held the receiver in my hand after he'd already hung up, but when I heard the annoying beeping sound in my ear, I put it down. It was like the sound woke me from a dream. No, worse, a nightmare. I felt like my best friend, who I told all my secrets to and loved more than my own brother, stabbed me in the heart and left me to the scavengers. My heart broke into a million pieces, and all that was left of me was an empty shell.

I went down to school the next day in a rage of fury with only one thing in mind. I wanted to hurt Shawn for all the pain he had caused me.

I had never been in a real fistfight before, so I was feeling a bunch of mixed emotions. I'm not the fighting type, and I didn't want to hurt him. Yet, I was so mad that that's all I could think about doing. The emotions I was feeling all converged in my stomach, where they churned and created butterflies. And when the time came for me to actually do some hitting, I couldn't do it. I knew he wouldn't hit me back by the look in his eyes. At that point, I realized that he was still my friend, and that he was hurting as much as I was.

Time passed (about two weeks), and we started talking again. Gradually, we started to hang out together and do the same things we used to do. We came to see that we were so much alike that we needed each other to be ourselves. We were outcasts and, in spite of everything, we were friends.

Memories of the Past

KIM TARANTO

Sharing all our dreams and passions,
And making memories with crazy fashions,
Caring for each other with great affection,
We used to have a strong connection.

Laughter and tears from joy and pain,
She was the one who kept me sane.
We were sure of one thing only,
Our friendship stood for one and only.

Many crushes over the years
Had kept at bay our teenage fears.
We craved the one who'd be so kind,
The one we knew we'd someday find.

Yet through it all we never thought
We might get hurt by what we sought.
And though we thought we were so smart,
We weren't at matters of the heart.

But after months of quiet pain,
I apologized for being vain.

Although not worth a friendship lost,
I knew exactly what the cost.

Sometimes people have to change,
Their lives might have to rearrange.
But the experience that will last
Makes the memories of the past.

A Fact of Life

Whenever someone or some group is popular, there will always be jealousy and envy from other people and other groups. That is just a fact of life.

—KIMBERLY KIRBERGER

The Betrayal of a Friend

Few things hurt more than the betrayal of a friend, especially if it comes from a friend whom you have trusted and with whom you have allowed yourself to be vulnerable. It is hard to say what makes a friend turn against a friend. If you have been lied to or deceived by someone you trusted, know that it isn't your fault.

I once had a friend turn on me, and I could not for the life of me figure out why. It seemed completely random. She refused to speak to me, thereby making it impossible for me to ask her what the reason was for her behavior. I suffered so much. She did her best to convince everyone that I was some kind of monster and that hurt even worse. It was like I was fighting an invisible battle. I knew things were being said behind my back, but no one was talking honestly about what was going on.

—KIMBERLY KIRBERGER

King of the Mountain

JAKI GRIER

I may be little but,
  I
    WILL
      GROW
and this is something you should know.
This child you pick on while at play . . .
will be the one on top someday.
'Cuz I'm too cunning, strong-willed and wise,
to be
  held
    down
by tormentors' ties.
Sneers and jeers throughout the years have only made
  me stronger,
to keep both feet on solid ground, to stand up one day
  longer.
So tease me 'cuz I'm poor or strange, poke fun of
  clothes I'm made to wear.

And all the while,
　I smile, I smile,
　　　on through my day and on my way . . .
　　without the slightest care.

We Deserve a Friend We Trust

When we say we trust a friend, what we usually mean is we know our friend won't talk about us behind our back. We know he or she is truthful with us. We know our friend has our best interests at heart. These are things we deserve from a friend.

—KIMBERLY KIRBERGER

Rudolf

HEATHER VANHOOSE

Rudolf was a lonely reindeer,
All because his nose was red.
How could he stand his life?
It seemed so filled with dread.

Because of his nose,
They tormented him daily,
Chanting, name-calling,
Dancing so gaily.

All that horrible fuss
Over one little red nose!
But that's how kids are,
Even fawns, I suppose.

They got a laugh
At poor Rudolf's expense,
Dropping and building
Their own false pretense.

Well, the reindeer aren't real,
But I understand Rudolf's nose.
It's hard to be liked
When one part of you glows.

Jealousy Is a Painful Emotion

Everyone enjoys having friends who are good-looking, smart and attractive to the opposite sex. It is fun to be part of a group that is well-liked and popular. However, just like with anything in life, there are times when having attractive friends will present problems. Yes, I am talking about that green-eyed monster: jealousy. We have all had the moment when the guy we have been thinking and talking about nonstop walks right past us and up to our best friend. Or the time we begged our friend to try out for the play so we wouldn't have to do it alone and she gets the part that we wanted. These situations and ones like it are devastating. They are especially difficult because they are happening between you and someone you care deeply about.

The situations I mentioned above are ones where the friend is innocent and didn't deliberately try to hurt you. There are other situations where friends are more responsible for the outcome. For instance: You notice your friend is always flirting with your new boyfriend or she is always putting you down around a group of girls that she knows you already feel insecure around. For guys a common one is making fun of a friend in front of the very girl he wants to impress or bragging about achievements that you know are the weaknesses of your "friend."

It is much more painful when a friend purposely tries to make you jealous than when it happens in a more innocent way. Yet no matter how you slice it, jealousy is a painful emotion. Don't feel guilty when you feel jealousy. Just know that the best thing is to first allow yourself to feel it and, second, make decisions about what you want to do about the friends who are purposely trying to make you feel this powerful emotion.

—KIMBERLY KIRBERGER

Popsicles and Sticky Fingers

LIA GAY

I walked into Ashleigh's house for the first time in two years. In an instant my mind wandered back to the two of us at thirteen. I was flooded with memories of afternoons spent eating Popsicles and talking about boys on her kitchen floor. I could picture us there, our skinny little bodies against the cold linoleum, the closeness I had felt with her in those moments. I looked over at her now, my perfect opposite, and I immediately tried to retrace the road that had taken us to this spot, this exact spot where it had all began.

The beginning of our friendship was simple and sweet, as most are at that age. We were thirteen and, to us, the most important things were each other, our weekly sleepovers and our constant, yet never fulfilled, search for our first boyfriends. We would sit together on her kitchen floor for hours on end, eating Popsicle after Popsicle, and analyzing little moments from our week at school. Sleep on those coveted overnights would come reluctantly for us and only after our conversations had digressed to mere mumbles and nonsensical ramblings.

The eighth-grade dance weighed heavily on our minds during that time, and the thought of dates both excited and mortified us. We shopped for dresses together and ended up talking our parents into buying us similar ones from the same shop. Finally, after weeks of worry, Ashleigh had found a date and I hadn't. She promised me that I shouldn't worry; that I could come with the two of them and we would have as much fun as we always had together. As she promised, I did feel included, even though looking back I was probably a third wheel. Ashleigh and I took more pictures together than she took with her date. She assured me that high school was right around the corner, and that there would be a world of new opportunities for our friendship and our boyfriend search.

As promised, freshman year did stir up a new boyfriend for me. He was a sweet boy and I felt very close to him for some time. But something happened to Ashleigh once I became the first to actually have someone to call a "boyfriend." She didn't call as much, and our sleepovers became few and far between. I would try to talk to her about things, but it seemed like there was no joy in her voice for me anymore. She didn't want to talk about my boyfriend and me, which was clear from her complete lack of interest in any situation that involved his name or his likeness. She said she liked him and that she was happy for me, but it was obvious that something bitter was stirring inside her, and I couldn't figure out what it was.

I started to feel guilty. Ashleigh was looking at me differently and constantly criticizing my actions. I began to feel like somehow I was the bad friend. Maybe I wasn't giving her enough attention or I was too wrapped up in my other friends or my boyfriend. I tried to plan sleepovers or fun things to do that I thought would clear up the anger and hurt building between us, but they never quite worked out. There was always something wrong with our friendship or something about me that she disapproved of. Not only did I become dissatisfied with our friendship, but I also began to dislike myself. Why couldn't I be selfless like Ashleigh, who had given up so much and made me feel so included years ago? Now we were spending the majority of our time talking *about* each other, rather than to each other.

We rode this roller coaster through most of high school and a pattern began to develop. When I didn't have a boyfriend, things drifted back into some semblance of normal. We would grow close again and then the second I would start to date someone, we would drift apart. I tried to understand it, to do things differently, to make her feel better somehow, but with all the "trying" I grew tired.

Eventually I settled into a relationship with the same boy for the rest of high school and Ashleigh grew to like him. Yet, even though she liked my boyfriend, she still didn't seem too fond of me. She would leave me out of things, making sure I wasn't invited to parties, and even going out with groups of friends she knew I would not become involved with. It was sad because I could see in her eyes that she was longing for the same thing I was—love and acceptance from the other—but neither one of us knew how to say that. I don't even know if I knew I felt it at that time. On the surface we looked to be close—we went to prom in the same group and still passed notes and shared some good times together—but in our hearts there was no loyalty. There was no love for each other anymore and I missed her. Even with her right by my side, I missed her.

Ashleigh and I both chose out-of-state colleges. We knew, yet never discussed, the fact that we would no longer live just a few blocks away from each other. I think we both knew that our friendship had lost its strength. I knew we were not strong enough to survive the distance. The truth is, I don't even know if we wanted to.

A year went by and we talked very seldom—a few phone calls here and there, and an e-mail every once in a while. We made new friends at our new schools. I still had her pictures up in my room, and during my second year of college I decided to send Ashleigh a birthday card. I missed the thirteen-year-old Ashleigh and I hoped that maybe something in her had changed. In truth, I didn't write the card for her; I wrote it for both of us, hoping it might rekindle the part of her that had loved me at one time.

Two weeks later I received a response. It read, "I don't know what you want, but if it is to be my friend again you could have called. One card doesn't change two

years, Lia, and if you want to talk to me you can call me."
I was dumbfounded. I couldn't believe her response. It
was not what I had expected. But a gift isn't an expec-
tation; it's a gift. So I called her. I figured things could
not get much worse.

The phone call was not what I had expected, either.
Ashleigh actually sounded happy to hear from me. She
told me she had a boyfriend now and we talked for hours
about how they had met and what he was like. It had
finally happened for her, and that brought me joy. I had
just broken up with the same boyfriend I had been with
since high school. And after I explained our breakup, I
heard something in her voice I hadn't heard in seven
years: compassion. She was now the one with the boyfriend, and I was the one who was alone. All the times
she had told me that girlfriends are forever and boyfriends are fleeting now made a little more sense.

Standing in her kitchen did not bring back all the old
pain or the hurt or the jealousy. It brought back the most
innocent memories of us as children. Ashleigh and I are
still not best friends—at least we don't call each other
that anymore. We don't have sleepovers. We don't even
talk to each other once a week. What we do have are
those memories of sticky Popsicle fingers, and the
knowledge that friendships can be fleeting, too. It's the
memories you choose to keep and the lessons friends
teach you that stay with you.

Nine

Friends in Trouble

I have many friends who have found themselves struggling with difficult life decisions. I do not always agree with what they do or think the choices they make are the right ones, but I do try to be there for them. I have been happy and surprised to later find out how much my support has helped them.

Christine Kalinowski

Friends in Trouble

Sometimes it is hard to know what a friend needs, especially when a friend is making bad choices for himself or herself. There are those who think people have to make their own mistakes before they learn, but what if you decide to say nothing and a friend ends up in a fatal car accident or in the hospital? There are no easy answers to this question. Some suggestions would be:

- Always speak *your* truth. Whether your friend is ready to hear it or hates you for saying it, it is for your own sake that you have to say how you feel.
- Trust your instincts. If you feel that a friend is in serious trouble, do not be afraid to act on it. Nothing feels worse than wondering later what you could or should have done.
- If your friend is intent on self-destruction and you have done and said all that you can, sometimes you just have to separate yourself from your friend until he or she gets it together.
- Do your best to practice compassion rather than judgment. Judgment is negativity, and negativity

doesn't help anybody. Compassion, on the other hand, is realizing that we are all in this together and loving thoughts are the ones that will essentially heal us all.

[See back of book for hotline numbers.]

A Long Overdue Letter

LAURA TANGUAY

To my best friend,

This is my long overdue letter to try and right all the wrongs that I have done. I was never able to express to you how I felt about what you were going through. There is no training to prepare you to watch your best friend place her child up for adoption. This is my apology for not being the best friend that I should have been and my attempt to be that best friend now.

About two and a half years ago you told me you were pregnant—on my sixteenth birthday. I have wondered why you chose to tell me then, with other people around. Were you afraid of my reaction and chose a time when I could not react? I admit; I didn't react. And perhaps I still haven't.

I was afraid to say anything. I always supported you, even if I didn't say it in words. It bothered me that other people could so openly ask you anything. Here I was, your best friend, and I could not even bring myself to ask you if you were keeping the baby. For some reason, I was too afraid. I was so worried about saying the right thing that

I didn't realize that saying nothing at all was even worse.

I know that deciding to place the baby up for adoption was the hardest thing you have ever had or will ever have to do. Yet, I couldn't even ask you how you were doing. And that bothered me. I talked with other people about my inability to be there for you. They told me to be there for you and talk to you. That made me even madder for some reason. No one seemed to understand why it was so difficult for me. To this day I don't even know why.

Everyone constantly asked me about my reaction to your pregnancy. They also wanted to know what I thought you should do about it. I managed to avoid the questions by saying that I supported you in whatever you did. And I did, even if I never told you. It was not until a few months ago that I realized what I had been doing. By not talking to you about what was going on, I was staying unattached. I did not want to become attached to that little baby. It hurt too much to be close. I knew that you were going to go through an extremely painful time when you had to give that baby up, and selfishly I did not want to go through that pain with you. And now I wish I had.

I have so many regrets. I never felt him kick. I never got to hold him and tell him that his Auntie Laura loves him very much. I never took a picture of him. I never finished the baby quilt I was making for him. And I never gave it to him. Instead, it sits in my hope chest, underneath a scrapbook containing his birth announcement. I never apologized to him for being a horrible best friend to his mother. And that is my biggest regret of all—not being there for his mother.

I wish that I could turn back time, but I cannot. If I could, I would be a better best friend. I am sorry I was distant and appeared like I didn't care. I cared more than you will ever know, but I was terrible at expressing it. I do not deserve to have you as a best friend. You have treated me so much better than I have treated you.

I am at a loss for words. I have written this letter a hundred times before, in a hundred different ways, yet none sounds better than the one before. I need to find a better way to tell you how sorry I am for not being a better friend. Maybe that is how I do it. Maybe that is the simplest way to say it.

I am sorry.

Love,
Laura

Suffering Is a Part of Life

One of the most difficult things to accept about life is the fact that suffering is a part of it. People die, get sick, hurt each other and hurt themselves. One of the most important lessons I have learned is that it is very important to accept the bad with the good, the light with the dark and the pain with the joy. I have learned that without pain I wouldn't know joy. I have learned that because of things like illness and death it is that much more important to love and live life to the fullest. Great lessons are learned from terrible tragedies, tremendous growth takes place when we are pushed to our very limits, and although I don't necessarily like the "tough stuff" I am learning to live with it.

—KIMBERLY KIRBERGER

My Beautiful Loss

ZOË GRAYE

Sometimes I find myself floating between memories of you and our times together. I resent you, Jessica, for leaving me like this. I miss you, Jes, for not being with me on my birthday and the senior prom, or just to sit and laugh with. You always gave me giggles. I love you, Miss Jessie, for all that you were in my life and all that I will forever remember you as. But you are gone now, and all I have are the memories you engraved within me, and the note that you left on my car that night.

As long as I could remember it had been you and me—Jessica and Zoë. We met in kindergarten. Our moms had sent us both to school without our lunches, and we were escorted to the office to call them. From that moment on we were inseparable—two opposites who attracted, the best of friends.

We were different, you and I. You were beautiful, so full of life and sweetness. I highly admired you, Jessica. You were the one who everybody wanted to be, the brilliant beauty, rich with goodness. Do you remember the time that I got stood up for the Winter Formal and you forced me to go with you and your date? Do you remember? You danced every slow dance with me. That was the kind of person you were—selfless and caring. I was never really anything special, decent grades, gangly body, insecure. I was never what people called a head-turner like you, Jessica.

So then, what was it? What threw you over the edge? We all hear the stories about the girl who had everything, the girl like you, the girl you were. You took your own life exactly two years ago. You had just turned sixteen. We were sophomores in high school, still the best of friends. I found your note at dusk, just as the sun began to fade beneath the clouds in beautiful oblivion. The sunset that evening is something I will never forget. Its brilliance rests against the shock I endured while reading your letter.

My dearest Zoë,

By the time you read this, I will be gone. No, not out-of-town gone, but out of the world, out of existence and out of your life. I wish I could explain to you why. I wish I could hold you before I go. I wish I was as strong and brave as you, but the truth is, Zoë, I am not. You know me more than anybody, and yet there is so much inside me that you do not even know. I love you, Zoë, and I am so very sorry. Take care of yourself. Thank you for being my best friend.

Yours always,
Jessica Herrara

These last two years have been somewhat surreal. My grades went way down, and for a while I even thought about being selfish and following you. You have no idea how many people you hurt, how many hearts are broken because of what you did. You were my best friend. I would have died for you, given you all that I had, and I guess in a sense I did. You killed me in more ways than you killed yourself.

I am doing okay these days, healing slowly, but healing nonetheless. I have a boyfriend; his name is Danny. I am even doing fairly well in math. Remember how terrible I used to be?

Some days I lie on my back and look up into the sky hoping to, perhaps, see your face. I do not know what happens when we die. Do we become angels? I don't know. Jessica, I don't think I want you to be mine. I had you once, and you betrayed me.

I still don't understand, dear Jessica, why you had to pull the cord on your life. What was so awful? The beauty of a friendship like ours was that we could tell each other everything. If only I would have known, if only you would have told me.

I am graduating this summer, Jessica. I am going off to college, English major. You wanted to study English, too, remember? You inspired me. You inspired so many, and then left us all, so selfishly.

In the evening, when I look out onto that beautiful sunset, out and into oblivion, I am sorry. I am sorry because you cannot see the beauty of life anymore; you cannot feel the warmth enrapture you. I watch as the sun disappears. And I feel blessed to be alive, to endure what you could not. I have finally let go, but Jessica, I don't know if I will ever forgive.

No Truer Gift

KATHY PONCHER

She died; I wasn't ready.
I suppose one never is.
I wept, my heart so heavy
Full of pain so desolate.

Yet all the while a distant thought
Was welling up inside.
My pain was building walls
Wherein my heart could hide.

Safe from the place of no more smiles,
No clever spoken lines,
No reading of each other's thoughts,
No warm hands soft in mine.

No truer gift could be bestowed,
Nor could it have been script.
For in these walls were stored the jewels
Of our true friendship.

♥

Suicide Is *Not an Option*

Suicide is the third leading cause of death among people ages fifteen to nineteen, and the second leading cause of death among those nineteen to twenty-four. Suicide is a real thing and it is, in my opinion, the saddest and most tragic type of death. I had a very dear friend end his life, and I will never fully recover from the pain of it. I can't tell you how many letters I receive from teens who have lost a friend to suicide or who are considering suicide themselves. What would make a person decide that death is the best option is something I have never understood, and in some ways I think that makes me unqualified to comment on it. I do know many people who have attempted suicide, and they have told me that there was a moment when they became terrified of dying. Of course, these are the ones who have lived to tell about it, but it is important to know this. Imagine if you did something to end your life and suddenly you wanted more than anything to live . . . but it was too late.

I think we need to remove the possibility of suicide from our minds, from our vocabulary. We need to decide it is simply <u>not an option</u>.

—KIMBERLY KIRBERGER

Please, Don't Leave Me Now

CHRISTINE LEGGETT

When you feel there
is nothing else to live for,
a friend gives you reasons.

Shawn Hauser

I went through a rough patch during my junior year in high school. I felt that there was no way out, so I almost committed suicide. When I told my best friend Christine, she wrote me this letter. I never realized what an impact I had made on her life, and I never would have imagined how deeply she would come to affect mine.

Dear Sue,

There is so much that I want to say to you right now. I don't even know how to put it into words, and I don't know where to start. When you told me of what you were thinking of doing, my heart stopped. Just the thought of you being gone from my life is too much for me to bear. You said to me last night that I cry too easily and that I don't have anything to cry about. The truth is that my life was flashing before me when you told me, and I didn't like the way it looked without you there.

In middle school, I had never felt accepted by Hannah or Dana. They both were so different from me. They were smart and played sports. I was the shy new girl that they had "taken in." I wasn't happy with myself, and I was self-conscious of what other people thought of me. Then you came into the picture and made my life so much better. With you I felt accepted. You made me feel good about myself and more confi-dent. Together we grew and expanded our horizons. We grew close, and together we found even more people we could call our friends.

As we got older you became my best friend, someone that I felt close enough to call my "sister." You are the person who I can always talk to and feel at home with. You are the one who helped me to find my first boyfriend. But boyfriends come and go, as you know, and friends are forever.

What would my life be like if you weren't in it? Who would I cry to when I was having a really bad day? Who could I play chubby bunny with or play Monopoly with on a warm, sunny day? Who could I order a number-two at McDonald's with, without feeling bad about the thousand grams of fat I was consuming? Who could I go to Dunkin' Donuts and get a hot chocolate with? Whose house could I have a slumber party at and still feel like I am at home? Who would I laugh with over the memories we have shared?

I look further into the future and see an empty spot at my wedding where my maid of honor is supposed to be. I see an empty spot at my child's baptism where her godmother is supposed to be. And I see an empty spot at the dinner table where my best friend would sit.

By taking your life you would be taking a huge piece of mine. You are loved so much by so many, and you have so much going for you. You have your health, your boyfriend, your family and, most of all, your friends. We will always be there for you, through thick and thin, the good times and bad. We'll face things together. You have a bright future ahead of you. Please don't let your life be cut short because of a test that means nothing or a fight with your boyfriend. It isn't the end of the world, although it may seem that way at the time. No matter how hopeless things may seem, there is always a light at the end of the tunnel.

When you come to a crossroads in your life, you must choose which way you will turn. When you feel that you have reached a dead end, search in your heart and you will find the right path. Things will work out, they always do, and I will always be there beside you to help you guide yourself to the right path. We're in this together. Please, don't leave me now.

Friends forever,
Christine

Could I Have Helped Them?

Whenever you talk to someone who has lost a friend to suicide the person always remarks, "I wonder if I could have helped them. Maybe if I had stayed by his side," or "why didn't she call me?" Someone once referred to it as being plagued with the "what ifs." However, we might never know about the times a friend came to us and we <u>did</u> save his or her life.

If you have a friend who is suffering or who has expressed suicidal thoughts, remember this is serious. Think to yourself: If this person actually did kill himself or herself, what would I regret not doing? Don't be afraid to go to an adult for help. Don't hesitate to get others to help you as well. You shouldn't take this on by yourself.

At the same time, I beg of you not to threaten suicide as a way to get attention. I worry that so many people talk about ending their life when they are upset that we are getting numb to it.

If you want to make a difference, make a pact with your friends that you won't consider suicide, you won't threaten suicide and you won't ever use the word lightly. As part of the pact also agree to be there for each other when things become really hard. The reality of how many teens we are losing to suicide is just too sad. If you have any ideas of how to help, please act on them.

[See back of book for suicide hotline numbers and resources.]

—KIMBERLY KIRBERGER

The Ribbon

CANDY RHODES

"I have leukemia." Those were the first words out of Blake's mouth after I answered the phone.

"What? You're lying to me," I replied, praying that he was.

"Candy, I have leukemia. Why would I lie about something like this?" At that moment, I burst into tears. He tried to tell me he would be okay, that he was strong. But it was so hard for me to understand. Why does this happen to the best people, the ones who haven't even lived their lives?

The next day at school, my friend Jessica handed me a red and blue ribbon, the kind you get off a perfume package.

"Blake came over yesterday, and he told me to give this to you. He said maybe you could wear it in your hair," she told me, handing me the ribbon. I looked at it for a minute and shrugged my shoulders, putting it inside my pocket.

A month later, Blake was at a hospital about two hours away from where we lived. I begged my dad every weekend to take me to see him, and finally one day he told his boss he had to take the afternoon off. I was thrilled.

I wanted to give my best friend a gift. But what? I pulled the ribbon out of my dresser drawer, found some scissors and clipped it into two pieces. I put one in my front pocket and stuffed the other in an envelope, along with a letter explaining it to him. I told him to keep his half beside his bed, and I would keep mine near me, too. I went into the hospital that day with a grin on my face the size of Texas. As I scrubbed my hands with disinfectant, I wondered if the ribbon would mean anything to him. I walked in the tiny room and took in his presence for a second before I ran over to give him a long, hard hug. I handed him a teddy bear and the envelope. He opened the envelope and looked up at me.

"What is this?" he asked, a little bewildered.

"Just read the letter," I told him.

We talked for a while and then he started looking tired, so I told him that I had to leave and for him to get some rest. All the way home I held the ribbon close to me. That night, as I pulled off my jeans, I remembered the ribbon still in my pocket. I took it out and folded it around my finger. And that is where it stayed all night. For the next four months, the ribbon was with me everywhere I went: school, home, shopping, at friends' houses, church and in bed. Where I went, it went. It was something to remind me that I had a great friend who would be home very soon. Blake said that he wore his around his arm and sometimes kept it in his nightstand.

He had it close to him when he was being tested and treated and poked and prodded, when he lay scared at night that he might never get better and in the early morning when he was thankful for another day.

Finally, Blake came home! I was so happy. We went to see a movie. It was indescribable. That night, the ribbon was still in my pocket. I had a feeling it would never leave, that I would never let go of what had kept me sane during that time we were apart. And I haven't.

Thank You, My Friend

NELLIE MCDOWELL

Thank you my friend
for just being you.
For just being there
when I needed you.
For giving and giving
without a reprieve.
For giving me someone
to trust and believe.
You gave me your shoulder,
your ear and your heart.
And by this you kept me
from falling apart.
You shared with me some
of your wisdom and mirth
And made me feel like
I was someone of worth.
Because you were there
I will always be grateful.
And because you're my friend,
I will always be thankful.

My Secret

DANIELLE GLICKSON

When I heard the 11:48 bell at school, I knew it was time for lunch. I pried my brown paper lunch bag open. I carefully unwrapped my sandwich, took in a huge breath and took a bite. Then I slowly finished the rest of the lunch. I felt full, and that wasn't a feeling that I liked. I excused myself from the lunch table and strolled down the empty hallway to the bathroom. Once in the stall, I stood over the toilet shaking. Deadlines, teachers, arguments with friends, comments that boys had made about my body and the standards I set for myself all swirled around in my head as I bent over slightly, and shoved my finger down my throat. I gagged twice. I quickly flushed, washed my hands and ran back to the lunch table.

This routine went on for many months. No one really caught on to my secret, and that was the way I wanted it. On the outside, I was skinny Danielle, always smiling, popular, nice to everyone, smart and without a care in the world. To most people, I was perfect. To myself, I was nothing.

I was in control of myself for the next six months. I felt good knowing I could make any problem vanish. All I had to do was throw up, and the problem would suddenly disappear. It was a good feeling.

One night, I lost all self-control. I was in the mood to just fall over and sleep forever in my cozy bed when all of a sudden my mom barged in and started asking me all these questions. My head started to spin and I snapped. I began to scream at my mom like never before, saying things I now regret. I even kicked her to get her out of my room. When I finally shut my mouth, I looked her in the eyes. I saw how hurt and upset she was. As tears filled my eyes, shame filled my heart. She turned around and walked out of my room.

That night I threw up three times. I couldn't fall asleep so I sat in bed just thinking. I still couldn't believe what I had done that night. I realized that what I was doing to myself was wrong. I was not only hurting myself, but I was hurting everyone who cared about me as well. I took out a pen and paper, and began to write. I started the letter with, "Dear Paige . . . I have something to tell you . . . I just can't hide anymore." I knew that was the right place to start. It felt like the best thing I'd done in a while, and I was back in control. Paige was my best friend. She was sweet, always there for me, and I trusted her with my life.

The next day I gave Paige the carefully written letter. In the middle of the day, she came up to me crying. She gave me a big hug and, at that moment, I knew everything would be all right. She ended up telling Jessica and Stacie, two of our other close friends. I never knew how much they cared about me, but looking back I couldn't have made it without them.

About a week later, I was called down to the guidance office. Paige, Jessica and Stacie had been worried, so they had told a counselor. I met with Christy. She was a very sweet lady and really guided me in the right direction. She explained to me that I needed to tell my parents what had been going on over the past year. That scared me a little, but I knew it was the next step to my recovery. I told my parents in a letter; I had good practice with that. Once they were informed, Christy called my mom. They signed me into the best eating-disorder program in Minnesota.

The first day was horrible. I had to spend the entire day at the clinic. Doctors asked me all sorts of questions and poked around at my slender body. After that visit, I had to make weekly three-hour visits to the clinic. I hated going there and threw fits before I had to go. But I knew it was the only thing to do, so I went.

A year later, I completed my clinic visits and had recovered from my eating disorder. I was a fast recovery case because I got help early on. I had bulimia. But I was lucky enough to realize my problem before I binged and purged myself to death. I am a strong fighter. And I have the greatest friends. My friends and my family helped keep me alive.

Eating Disorders

Our society holds beauty ideals for young girls that are almost impossible to meet. The super-models that we see plastered all over magazines are paper-thin and look half-starved. Girls and young women can easily get the idea that to be thin is to be beautiful and that, as the stupid saying goes, "You can't be too rich or too thin." Well, guess what? You can. It's very hard to have a healthy self-image in a world that constantly tells you that you have to starve yourself to be attractive. If you recognize yourself as a person who struggles with negative body image, to the point where you cannot consume food without feeling horribly guilty or making yourself throw up, please seek help immediately. Remember that you are not alone and help is out there.

Also, from a guy's point of view, healthy bodies are much better than "paper-thin, half-starved" ones.

[See back of book for eating disorders hotline numbers and resources.]

—Colin Mortensen

"I can't find a good photo for my Web page.
Every picture of me looks too much like me!"

Reprinted by permission of Randy Glasbergen.

Friends in Trouble

If you have a friend who has talked about suicide or who you suspect has an eating disorder, don't try to handle the situation by yourself. No one should have to shoulder that kind of responsibility alone. Besides, these are situations that require professional help.

We have heard many stories of teens' lives being saved because they had a friend who cared enough to get help for them. Even though it is really scary and you are afraid that your friend will hate you for telling his or her secret, when someone's life is on the line, all bets are off.

—KIMBERLY KIRBERGER

I Can't Feel Elley Anymore

TRACEY R. GRIMM

I see you wedged there,
in that dark, tiny crevice.
Stuck, where my arms can't reach you.
I can almost touch you, but
you just keep digging yourself deeper
into this pit of despair that is
uncompassionately holding you captive
and muffling your scream,
squelching it
to that of a hoarse whisper,
which I alone can hear.
I can't help you anymore.
All I can do is give you a Band-Aid.
A temporary fix,
though you know I'd give my life
just to be able to extract you
from your hopeless prison.

I simply can't.
It's beyond what my flesh can do.
Oh, my friend, please remove your gag
and scream at all your chains.
Rise up, stand tall and free yourself,
for the only thing that's holding you down
is the soul-killing pain that you inflict on yourself.
Please, my friend, find your wings and come fly with me.

Stop the Cycle of Abuse

Individuals who are abused at one time or another in their lives have to work a million times harder to make their relationships or friendships functional and healthy. As emotional beings we have a tendency to recreate our dysfunctional patterns in our current friendships and relationships. For example, if a person's parents are abusive that person is much more likely to seek out an abusive lover or friend. This way of relating is familiar and comfortable to them. You don't have to be a victim of abuse; please seek the help of a trusted adult who has the power and resources to work on your behalf.

—COLIN MORTENSEN

One Final Lesson

NOAH CAMPANA

One rainy day I was at home playing on my computer when the phone rang. It showed up on my caller ID as one of my really good friends from across the state. I anxiously grabbed for the receiver and answered. But instead of the lively reply that I had come to expect from my friend, I heard nothing but sobbing. She was crying so hard she couldn't even talk. Finally she got it all out. Two of her best friends had just died. Slowly over the next hour and a half I got the story piece by piece.

After I hung up I couldn't clear my mind of what I had just heard. It was a scenario I had heard too many times in my life. So I pulled the facts together and wrote a story of what happened. The following is what I came up with.

The last day of school is today. It couldn't be more perfect since today is also your seventeenth birthday. All that you and two of your buddies have planned is a night out on the lake.

For a couple of hours you and your friends sit in a little aluminum boat in the middle of the lake under the colorful skies painted by a setting sun. As you guys empty can after can from a case of beer, you talk about the usual: girls and your plans for the summer, and what it's going to be like when school begins and all three of you are finally seniors.

You don't notice the wind beginning to pick up, churning the calm, smooth lake into something dangerous. By the time you realize it's time to come in, the waves have already begun to thrash your little boat. Your friend gets the engine going and handles the steering while you work the throttle. As soon as he gets the engine started you open the throttle, maybe just a little more than you should. With a jolt, the little boat is sent speeding across the waves. Halfway to the landing you helplessly watch in horror as you notice a huge wave coming at you from the side. Your friend turns the boat into the wind and toward the wave as you throttle down the engine for all you're worth, but not soon enough. The wave hits the boat at an angle, sending her off the crest and smashing down into its trough. All three of you are knocked against the side, as the force of the wave capsizes the boat and sends you all into the lake.

You kick for the surface but your legs feel heavy and sluggish. It feels as if something is pulling you down into the depths. Your boots, now weighted by the water, are pulling you deeper and deeper into the darkness. As much as you try, the light of the surface becomes more and more distant. As your last few seconds of consciousness pass, you desperately try to pull your boots off. You tear at the laces but they won't come undone. You panic, thrashing wildly, doing anything just for a breath of precious air. Before blackness consumes you, images of your friends and family swim through your mind. *No,* you think to yourself. *This isn't happening to me. I'm only a teenager. I can't die!*

And then, almost as an answer to your thoughts, you miraculously find yourself on the sandy shore—dry, warm and sober. You see one of your friends swimming toward the beach. You call out to him, but he doesn't respond. He pulls himself out of the lake, and he stands there shivering as water drips from his T-shirt, looking at the overturned boat. He calls out for you and your friend. "Hey!" you yell as you walk over to him. "I'm right here." But he doesn't seem to notice. He calls out again, and again you give him your same response: "Hey! I'm right here!" You step in front of him but his frantic eyes look past you, around you and even through you.

"Oh, God," he says to himself. "What have I done?" He takes a few steps backwards, then turns and runs up the road.

"Hey!" you yell. "Hey, where are you going?!" But it's almost as if you had said nothing at all. You watch helplessly as he continues to run until he disappears from sight.

For a time, all is silent. Ten minutes pass, then twenty. After thirty, maybe thirty-five minutes a siren pierces the silence. At first you don't notice. But within minutes ignoring it is impossible. Down the road come a multitude of emergency vehicles, followed in short succession by cars and trucks, some of which you recognize as belonging to friends. As people jump out of the cars you notice that your parents are there also. Your father walks somberly while your mother sobs endlessly in his arms. You run over to your parents, yelling out to them, but they don't seem to hear. They pull an officer aside to talk, to find out what is going on. As you get closer you hear the officer say, "Ma'am, I'm sorry, but your son's body is missing. We have called in helicopters to search the beaches with searchlights. Men on horseback have gone up to scan the cliffs . . . divers will come in tomorrow."

"But you don't need all of them!" you yell. "I'm right here! I'm not dead! It's not supposed to happen to me!"

As the night draws to a close, the lake fills with more and more boats. People from all over your little town are out on the water with flashlights, calling out for you and your missing friend. And no matter how hard you yell, no one seems to hear you. You walk by groups of some of your best friends, and even some of those people with whom you never really got along. Some of them are trying not to cry, yet holding those who are.

You watch your girlfriend crying and calling out for you as her friends try to comfort her. "Don't cry," your soundless voice says to her. "I'm not dead. I can't be. I'm only seventeen. This can't happen to me."

Night gives way to morning and no one has left; instead, more have come. Your mother is out on the dock. She has been there for nearly five hours. You watch as your father and an officer walk out to her and you hear your father whisper, "C'mon honey, it's time to go now." She breaks into tears while you try desperately to hold back yours. She won't go. Not until the body of her son is found. The flood of emotions hits you like a brick wall when the police have to sedate her in order to move her from the end of the dock. *This shouldn't be happening,* you tell yourself. *I'm only a teenager. I can't be dead.*

The names of you and your friend, which have been called out by rescuers all night long, are drowned out by the high-pitched roar of two army helicopters. Immediately, their searchlights pierce the fading darkness and begin sweeping over the lake and the beaches that surround it.

One of the searchlights passes overhead and you put your arms in front of your face as the blinding light engulfs you. And then the light is gone. . . .

You lower your arms and look around. The helicopters are gone, as are the police, medics and the firemen. They are all gone. The boats that once carried searchers and their flashlights bob gently in their moorings at the dock. Your friends no longer sit on the shore, crying at the realization that two of their companions are forever lost.

Instead, the sun rises over the clear and pristine lake. The sky is blue, with not a cloud in sight. Your clothes ripple as a cool west wind slips beside you.

In a clearing you can see a small congregation of people. As you walk closer, each and every one of them becomes familiar—each of them a friend or a family member. There are two sections of folding chairs, all of which are occupied. Before them, beside a little makeshift podium, propped above a pile of flower bouquets are two pictures: one is of your friend whom you never saw after the boat capsized and threw all three of you into the lake. You hesitate to look at the other picture because you already know—it's you.

As one friend leaves the little podium, another stands and takes his place. She speaks about what the two of you meant to her and how much she will miss you. One by one, friends and relatives come up to speak, each emphasizing how much you will be missed. And you sit there and watch. All the time not believing that it did happen to you. That you died, even though you were still a teenager.

These Days

JESSICA DOWDY

These days I think of Taylor.
Flying high with people she thinks are friends.
"I'm living my life to the fullest,
we only live once, right?" she says.
She wants to try anything,
and do everything.
She is unaware of the bags under her eyes,
or the slight tremble of her hands
when she thinks she's sitting still.
Taylor lives in a world of highs and lows.
As the lows get worse,
she craves the highs even more.
She makes sacrifices to feed her addiction.
Sometimes she wishes there were a way to escape,
to free herself.
But the steps to take are too high
and the ropes holding her are too strong.
I reach out to her,
but only our fingertips touch.
If only she would take one more step.

Surely drugs can be demolished for Taylor.

These days I think of Emma.
Burying her face in a pillow,
curled up in her bed, lying next to the wall.
She is afraid to breathe or move,
so she lays still and gasps for air only when she must.
"Stop it, Dad," she whimpers,
but Emma knows no one hears her.
She tightly closes her eyes and prays for it to be over.
She hears the cries of her mother and the rage of her
    father.
Somehow she blames herself.
If only she had the strength to stop it.
Some days she stands up and fights,
but it only makes it worse for her mother.
Where will she find a solution?
There's got to be a solution.
Her dad says that he loves her and that it's not his fault.
She thinks dads never lie.

Surely domestic violence can be stopped for Emma.

These days I think of Megan.
Standing in front of the mirror,
looking at herself.
Ribs pressing out against her skin,
her hip bones seemingly awkward and huge
compared to her tiny waist.
The dark circles under her eyes,
and the slightly yellow tint of her teeth.

But Megan doesn't see the person in the mirror,
staring back at her.
She sees someone who is ugly,
who will look okay once she loses a few pounds.
She craves compliments.
When people say, "You are so skinny"
the hunger inside of her dies down,
at least for a little while.
Megan tells them, "I'm not hungry" or "I already ate."
When she must eat, her stomach can't hold in her food
and she ducks into the bathroom.
Jogging, running, exercising in the rain and snow,
she must keep going.
Counting the calories,
and stepping on the scale each night.

Surely eating disorders can be cured for Megan.

These days I think of Alyssa.
Huddled in a corner.
Her eyes red and puffy,
her sleeves and collar soaked with tears.
The lights are dim
and her head rests against the cool wall.
Her long legs and bare feet are stretched out in front of
    her
and Sammy the teddy bear is tucked under her arm.
A half-filled glass of warm water sits on the floor next to
    her,
and has been there for the last two hours.
Her fingers are tightly curled around the little pills

that are resting in her sweaty palm.
Her ears strain for the sound of the telephone.
The voice of someone from school,
a person just wanting to talk.
But she knows that isn't going to happen.
Alyssa doesn't have many friends.
She reaches down and grasps the glass.
"I love you, Mom and Dad," she whispers.
Inside she feels empty
and the pulsating heart in her chest aches.
Her throat is dry and hoarse.
The raspy sound of her own breathing
makes her feel even more alone.
She doesn't want to be alone.

Surely suicide can be prevented for Alyssa.

These days I think of Hope.
I see her hurrying down the hall,
trying to dodge all the hateful glances.
People say things and frustrations run through her mind,
begging to burst out.
"What makes me so different from you?" she thinks,
but doesn't dare ask.
Hope already knows the answer.
It's the color of her skin,
the shell that is merely a cover to what's on the inside.
But no one wants to know her inner person,
they only see a face.
She clings to her family,
and depends on her "own kind."

She loses herself in music.
The voices have no color,
but the words speak out.
Hope wishes there were no black vs. white,
race vs. race.
She wishes people were seen only for who they are,
just people.

Surely racism can be ended for Hope.

These days I think of Ashley.
Fumbling through her purse,
pretending to search for chapstick,
but really trying to dig up the courage to face
what she is about to hear.
Her hands tremble and her lips quiver
as she blinks ever so softly.
The tears are welling up in her eyes
and could at any moment break through
and stream down her face.
Ashley realizes the consequences of her choices,
but doesn't fully understand what her punishment will
    be.
The long painful days and nights to come,
having to slowly watch the light inside her die.
She hears her heartbeat and wonders when
the day will come that it, too, stops.
She feels like she has just read the last page of a book
and now must go back and finish the few chapters before.
She wishes she didn't know and that somehow the book
    will be rewritten.

But, Ashley knows how the story ends,
and she says, "Never take life for granted."

Surely AIDS can be cured for Ashley.

These days I think of teenagers.
Struggling to overcome all of the obstacles life throws at
    them.
They are in a hurry to grow up, to become adults.
Adults who wish they hadn't grown up quite so fast.

Surely adolescence can be survived by all of us.

Ten

Growing Apart

*True friendship is like
sound health; the value of it is
seldom known until
it be lost.*

Charles Caleb Colton

Growing Apart

I have made many references to the difficulties you will face as teenagers. Growing up and apart from friends you have been close to for years is by far one of the most difficult.

As you get older you begin to figure out for yourself what your values and interests are. Oftentimes these will be very different from what you felt in earlier years. You are growing up and becoming an individual—your own person, so to speak.

This is all great, except for one thing: Your friends are doing the same thing. CHANGING.

The chances of you both changing in the same ways are very slim. It does happen but, more often than not, the changes that take place are ones that challenge the core of the friendship. Suddenly you are faced with the possibility of losing a friend who you thought you were going to have a double wedding with. If you are a guy, you may find yourself getting teased because you don't want to engage in the great idea your old best friend has just come up with.

Although there are no hard, fast rules for dealing with growing apart, there is some comfort in knowing that you aren't alone or at fault. As you will see in this chapter, many teens before you have gone through this and they have come out of it just fine. Sometimes that is the best that life has to offer: a good lesson here and a new friend there. In the end, you will be stronger and more appreciative of the friendships you get to keep.

Learning How to Be a True Friend

MELISSA COLLETTE

Always try your best. If there's a
weak spot, try to work on it as hard
as you can. Try to put all of your
effort and focus into it.

Joey of 'N Sync

Brooke and I were never what you would call "best
friends." We lived on opposite sides of town, went to different schools and had totally different friends. Yet somehow
we managed to stay close. My mom worked for her dad for
ten years, so through our parents and our occasional visits, we were informed of the major events in each other's
lives. It was always fun when we would see each other at
our rival schools' football games. When I found the "man of
my dreams," Brooke called to make sure he was taking

care of me. When Brooke was diagnosed with Hodgkin's lymphoma, my mom shocked me with the news and I was devastated. How could the star volleyball and soccer player, the awesome student, the perfect friend and the most beautiful girl I had ever had the privilege to know have cancer? All I could manage to do was cry.

The following week happened to be Brooke's seventeenth birthday and her surprise party. Everyone important in her life stopped by to celebrate and show his or her support. Her dad made a comment to me that night about how this would be the truest of all friendship tests. As he stood next to me and cried, he asked me to promise him that I would take good care of Brooke and visit her as much as possible. He reminded me that she was going to need a lot of love and support from those close to her, to keep her strong. I believed in my heart that I would keep my promise to him. I had no doubts at all that I was a true friend.

Days passed, and I hadn't made an effort to see or even call her. I excused my absence in her life by convincing myself that I was too busy. I knew how untrue and unfair that really was. Then weeks and months passed. As I had always known what was going on in Brooke's life from my mom, I was similarly kept up with her medical standing on a day-to-day basis. I continued to scold myself when I wondered how I was ever going to explain to Brooke why I had disappeared from her life. I was infuriated with myself when I ran into her boyfriend on campus and couldn't come up with any acceptable reason why I, one of Brooke's longtime friends, hadn't come to visit her in over ten months. And I was filled with despair every time her gorgeous brown eyes stared out at me from the picture of the two of us that sits on my entertainment center. My habitual neglect of our friendship constantly ate me up inside.

One night as my mom and I sat over dinner at our favorite restaurant, she told me that Brooke had found two new lumps. I was miserable. The last I had heard, she was doing quite well and was in remission. Now this. I couldn't even finish my dinner. I hadn't taken a single bite, but suddenly I felt overwhelmingly full. Ten million thoughts raced through my head at once as guilty tears poured down my cheeks and neck. I had always considered myself a "true friend," but now my perspective changed. Was I ever really a true friend?

After thinking it through, I discovered the reason that I had run from a closer friendship with Brooke. I was selfish, and I was afraid. I had never lost anyone close to me before. I was afraid of how I would deal with becoming closer to Brooke and then possibly losing her. I was selfish to worry about me, when it was Brooke who needed her friends now more than ever. I figured that everyone else must know how to deal with illness and loss, but I was wrong. I've learned that no one ever knows. But I continued to stay away.

What I wish I would have known sooner was that she didn't care if I didn't know exactly what to say or how to act. She didn't care if I couldn't visit all the time—we hardly saw each other before anyway. Sadly, she had come to realize that most people don't know how to deal with cancer. This was the "friendship test" that her dad was talking about, and I had failed miserably.

As much as I tried to convince myself that I was a true friend, I knew deep down in my heart that I wasn't. Would a true friend promise to be there for her companion and then never actually follow through? Would a true friend neglect to even call her sick friend to say hello? Would a true friend say she was "too busy" to visit? Would a true friend let her selfish fears of not knowing what to say or how to act around someone who has cancer get in the way of a friendship?

It took ten months, but I'm now finally taking the time to repair our friendship. Recently I put aside my fears and met Brooke for dinner—I'm taking it slowly. It was so good to see her. She looked fabulous! Her hair was shorter, but longer than I had expected it to be after months of chemotherapy. The best thing about her was that famous bright smile on her face and that special twinkle in her eyes. There are no words to express how much I admire her never-ending strength, courage and optimism while fighting such a difficult battle.

If only I could find the words to let her know how sorry I am. But, in a weird sort of way, I think she understands. Just like I understand how important my friendship is in her life and to her successful recovery. I know that I will never regret strengthening my friendship with Brooke, and I pray that her guardian angels will take extra-special care of her. More than anything else, I know that I wouldn't be able to live with myself if something should happen and I had neglected the chance to show her how much I love and care about her. I've had a lot of time to think, and it's like the saying goes: A true friend is one who comes in when the whole world goes out. From now on I want to be a "true friend."

Forget Guilt

Forget guilt because guilt is a useless emotion. It does nothing to improve the situation. If you have done something wrong or that you regret, take positive action. You can apologize, you can learn a lesson, you can change the behavior—you may even be able to reverse the action and right the wrong. Just be sure not to waste your time sitting around feeling guilty.

—KIMBERLY KIRBERGER

Losing Lola

ALEXANDRA ZISSU

**People grow and people change,
and that's something you
just have to accept.**

Jenny Sharaf

The summer Lola told me she was moving to Paris was the worst. I cried harder than I did when Josh broke up with me later that year.

I had met Lola the previous summer at camp. Although we were both from New York City, we didn't meet until we were in a cabin in the woods of New Hampshire. Lola was the coolest. She was beautiful. She wore a bra—and needed it! This was the summer before eighth grade, and she already had tons of boyfriends. She was so high school. She knew the latest music and fashions. She told me stories about smoking cigarettes and going out at night—to nightclubs!—in the city. I was in awe of this and her seemingly magical qualities. She could, for example, put oily Vaseline body cream on her face and not get pimples. She could even use cheap, drying mousse in her black curly hair and it still came out shiny and unfrizzy. No such luck for me. Basically, as girls tend to do at some point in their lives with another girl, I worshipped Lola. She was enthralling and rebellious and she knew just how to cut and wear jean shorts.

The relationship wasn't one-sided. She told me she loved things about me, too, and we sang James Taylor's "You've Got a Friend" really loudly together at campfires. But her friends from home were clearly more important to her. That made me feel bad about myself. When she made out with the boy I had a huge crush on that summer, she made sure to tell me all of the details. That also made me feel bad about myself. Looking back on it today, Lola wasn't all that nice to me. I had other camp friends who tried to explain that to me, but I just thought they were jealous of how much time I was spending with Lola, so I didn't listen to them.

I began to get angry with Lola when she hardly had time for me during the school year. But we went to separate schools and we were busy, I told myself. My other camp friends, meanwhile, had plenty of time for me. One time I met Lola and her friends and we hung out for the day. They made me feel insignificant. I remember feeling relieved when I left them.

When we got back to camp the summer before ninth grade, the tables had turned slightly. Lola needed me; her mother had married a French man and moved to Paris. And, as soon as the summer was over, Lola would head to Paris, too. I was so upset. But I was also determined to be a good friend and help her through this difficult time. I listened to her talk about her fears, about what she would miss most about home. I held her hand, kept her company. We laughed a lot. I admit I was jealous when letters from her school friends would get her going about how much she was going to miss them; she seemed to like them so much better than me. But I had my own life to lead. I had just gotten contact lenses and an adorable—older!—boy was interested in me. We would kiss at night down by the waterfront, and I would run back to the bunk and tell Lola all about it before bed. Of course, Lola did flirt with him on the last night of camp that year, but I was too upset about her leaving to pay much attention.

I was bummed out for weeks after Lola moved. I wrote her tons of letters. I even convinced my parents to send me to Paris to visit her. They speak French, and it was my favorite subject in school. They were really cool and thought sending me would help me develop a love of travel. Lola met me at the airport . . . with another friend! Juliette, a Canadian exchange student, liked to stay with Lola instead of with her French family, and Lola's parents didn't mind. I was so jealous, having traveled so far only to find I had to share Lola. Juliette was older and even more sophisticated than Lola. She drank wine and was friends with diplomats' daughters. She rode the Paris subway like it was the easiest thing ever. I felt so grown-up for coming to Paris alone but now compared to Juliette, I felt like a silly little girl. My clothes weren't right. I wasn't right. I remember one time crying in front of both of them and feeling so ashamed.

Paris saved me, though. It is more beautiful, enchanting and interesting than one thousand Lolas. Lola wasn't so nice to me that trip but she did give me a gift: One night we went to a really trendy club—my first! They taught me how to dance and, even as Lola and Juliette giggled and excluded me, I learned to stick up for myself in a new way, to enjoy myself even if I *was* essentially alone. When we left the club we went to a café, where I drank my very first cup of espresso. To this day, I can't remember what Lola and Juliette were babbling about, but I can still remember the taste and smell of that coffee and how grown-up I felt. It was a personal triumph. I refused to travel that far and mope. Sure, Lola didn't feel the same way about me as I felt about her. That hurt. Enormously. But I still have amazing memories of Lola and of that trip.

When I got home, Lola and I wrote less and less. One time I heard that Lola came to New York and didn't call me. I was really upset, but each time Lola came to town after that it hurt less and less. Sometimes we saw each other, sometimes we didn't. It usually wasn't much fun, which is why, when we finally lost touch, I didn't really mind.

You Are Worthy of Friendship

Why do some friendships stick while others fall apart despite a great effort to make them last?

The easiest thing to do when you lose a friend is to blame yourself and somehow feel that you just weren't good enough. This simply isn't so. There are so many things that determine whether or not a friendship lasts and, as in love, chemistry is one of them.

Try to trust in the fact that the friendships that are meant to be will be and the ones that are not won't. Also, trust in the fact that you are worthy of friendship and, if you lose it one place, you will certainly find it someplace else.

—KIMBERLY KIRBERGER

Once upon a Long Time Ago

PEGGY MILLER

We met at the age of four, the sun fertilizing our young bodies as we lay sprawled across the summer grass. We were as naive as could be and unaware of any other moment. The chlorine from hours of swimming had tinted our sun-streaked blonde hair a faint green. Kool-Aid had stained our pre-kindergarten lips with the colors of childhood.

Our days of pure enjoyment would soon come to an end, however. Kindergarten beckoned, and we weren't going to be in the same class. We were anxious about going but had already been through preschool, and so we weren't concerned with the fundamental matters.

In the mornings before afternoon kindergarten, Leigh and I sat together in front of *Sesame Street* characters that taught us to count to ten in Spanish. We each had a nutritious and delicious peanut butter and jelly sandwich with a cool, refreshing glass of milk. Afterwards, we met the bus with our moms, and they proudly snapped pictures as their babies ventured out into the world.

Leigh and I played together almost each and every hour. We spent many of our days under a cool shade tree in front of my house, molding figures with Play-Doh, as our youth soared away. We were rarely apart, and when we were, we could hardly wait for the other to return. Our daily separation lasted for exactly half an hour, while I had to practice my tedious piano lessons so my mother could entertain her visions of my life as the next Mozart. Though she could see me playing through the glass door, Leigh would knock on the door and wave every five minutes or so, just to be sure I hadn't finished and forgotten about her.

Every summer, we celebrated our birthday together. We would each have a birthday cake trimmed with six or seven or eight flickering candles, perfectly arranged on a creamy layer of fattening, bakery icing. Children stood impatiently while the birthday girls rapidly tore open their gifts. Bright smiles lacking baby teeth covered every child's face and all were joyous. Sweets, presents and friendship coated those moments to preserve them for a lifetime.

The summer before fourth grade, our family moved away. We didn't go far, but it seemed far to a nine-year-old. I can still hear Leigh's mother reassuring us that we would still be friends. Of course we were, but not nearly as close as we had been. Two years later, Leigh and I were reunited when we started sixth grade at the middle school.

We felt like babies amidst the older and bigger middle school kids. Fortunately, we had gym and science together. Most of my classes were more advanced, while Leigh chose to focus on her social life over her studies. When we ran for student council, Leigh made it; I didn't. Our colorful, creative posters filled the halls, and I even went so far as to hand out cute little paper bookmarks. People seemed to be interested, but the hallway floors were soon littered with my name. Leigh didn't need anything to promote her name. Everyone who knew her loved her. As she rose in popularity, she never acted too good for me. Although people in her new clique were "too cool" to talk to me, she always let me know that I was the coolest of all the members of the "nerd herd"—the smart kids.

High school is a lot different from middle school. People have changed a lot and the cliques are more solid and impermeable than ever. I'm on the soccer team and have made some new friends. Leigh is a cheerleader. She has new friends, too—football friends. When we talk, we mostly just share stories and memories from our past. Yesterday we reminisced about the innocence and freedom of our cartwheeling young bodies soaking up the warm sun. We miss those days; they live in both our hearts.

Lollipop Days

ALICE DODDS

Whatever happened to the
Lollipop days
Filled with sunshine and laughter,
That tasted as bittersweet
As fresh-squeezed lemonade?

Whatever happened to
Racing down the street on tricycles,
Running barefoot through ticklish grass
That had gone too long between mowings,
And whispering secrets
Behind the old sycamore tree?

Whatever happened to
Playing hand games 'til our hands
Were red and sore,
Or staying outside,
Bathing in the hot sun 'til
Freckles appeared on our noses?

Whatever happened to
That little girl
I used to call
My best friend?

We used to tell each other everything,
Now we barely talk.
We used to swing on these very seats
Until we reached the sky,
Now your swing lays empty
With nobody there to push it
Except the soft summer breezes.

They say things change,
They always do.
I know now
That must be true.

For never again will we
Giggle and whisper behind the
Old sycamore tree,
Or run barefoot through the grass.
Never again will a lollipop taste as sweet,
Or lemonade as bitter.

And never again will
We walk hand in hand
Down that long, empty dirt road
Called life.

When One Door Closes . . .

I've grown apart from friends who lived right next door and stayed close with friends who moved all the way across the country. While some old friends will go and new friends will come, the worst possible thing we can do is to grow apart from our own needs. Growing apart from friends—although painful—can often make room for new friends and new experiences.

—COLIN MORTENSEN

Gold Friend

MOLLIE F. DRABIK

When you have a good friend you want to keep her.
You see her every day.
You have special nicknames,
And funny things you like to say.
Then something happens as you grow older.
Interests change
Your lives do, too.
You don't see that friend as much as you used to.
You slowly drift apart,
Day by day,
Night by night.
You don't realize it,
But when you do
You start to write.
The first letter is long,
The one you get back is, too.
But neither remembers to write again
to the friend who wrote to you.
Time elapses,
Your mind forgets.

You start to drift.
Until you come across that letter,
The precious letter you saved.
And you think,
I wonder what she is doing today.
What has happened since I last wrote?
I wonder if she's made new friends,
And what friendships she has broke?
You remember the saying:
Make new friends, but keep the old.
One is silver, and the other gold.
You know she's a good friend,
You don't want to lose
So you take out some paper
And think of the right words to use.
You make an effort
To express to your friend
That friends of the heart,
You will be 'til the end.

Goofy Pictures Will Never Fade

CARMEN JOHNSON

It's amazing how fast a year flies by and how much things can change. Something so normal and obvious one year can seem so awkward and different the next. Take a regular, lazy Saturday afternoon. It's almost summer and you're flipping through the endless channels with your best friend. Munching on the last of the greasy chips, the two of you talk about the boring details of your day. Those terrible, corny "KOST 103.5" songs that you actually like are playing in the background as you scrounge for whatever types of junk food can be found in the depths of your kitchen cabinet. The thought of leaving the house is exhausting. That would require changing out of your comfortable pajama bottoms and old tennis T-shirt. More importantly, the brush would never make it through your uncontrollable mess of hair. You gossip with your friend about the exciting things happening in other people's lives and

discuss your weekend plans—hoping they will bring
something exciting to your life.

As the level of boredom grows, you decide to snap
some photos of your friend kissing the picture of Will
Smith hanging on your wall. Once you decide that Will
has had enough, you both fall asleep while watching a
low-budget, no-talent, never-gonna-get-an-Oscar movie,
your face in the popcorn. And all of this is fun.

Your friend has left but that doesn't mean you won't
talk to her for the rest of the day. Oh no, your mom can't
get any of her calls because you are upstairs on the
phone with a tightly closed door gossiping about the
same pointless yet *important* things you were just talking about five minutes before she left your house. You
manage to drown out your mom's yelling for you to get
off the phone because you're busy analyzing the smile
and "hello" she got today from the hottie in third period.
Before you have a chance to reach a conclusion on the
potential possibility of passing the next chemistry test,
your mom and dad have disconnected the phone.

I knew my best friend as well as I knew myself. We
could sense when something was wrong with the other
and were always finishing each other's sentences. I
never would have thought that our friendship could
change. How could we ever pass each other in the hallway without jumping straight into a lengthy discussion
about our last class? But I guess things do change.

Another year starts and zooms by before you know it.
One minute, I'm screaming with my best friend in the
hallways about the new guy in school, and the next

we're barely making small talk. No one ever really knows why things happen. Now, when I look at old pictures of us goofing around, it all seems so strange, as if we were different people. Now, the shallow small talk of "Hi, how are you?" always makes me think of the time when that was a pointless question. We either already knew or we'd dive right into it before the question was even asked. Nothing stays the same forever, and I guess I have to accept that. Friends will come and go just like a school year, but the goofy pictures will never fade.

♥

Your Hurt Will Make You Stronger

It is so hard to go through growing apart from friends, especially when you are the one being left behind and you don't even know why. The pressures of high school include how you look, if you are cool or not, who you are hanging out with and so on. Everyone falls prey to it to some degree. When what people think of you becomes more important than treating a friend "the right way" you have to question how shallow your friends are. No matter who you are, you will more than likely suffer from this superficiality at some point, and no matter who you are, it will most likely hurt. But try to keep it in perspective and remember that they are the ones being shallow. Know that your hurt will make you stronger and wiser, and spend your time and energy with people who know what real friendship is.

—KIMBERLY KIRBERGER

Losing Friends

LINDSEY ATAYA

You do not need to tell me,
That friends can grow apart;
That even the near and dear
May someday break your heart.

The ones that you love now,
Can't guarantee tomorrow;
And the ones that bring you joy,
May also bring you sorrow.

For although things may seem
Just perfect at the time,
People sometimes change,
And leave your heart behind.

You do not need to tell me,
I've been through it all enough,
I know just what it feels like
To lose someone that you love.

Whether it's a buddy or a pal,
A confidante or best friend,
It's the pain of losing them
That hurts too much to mend.

And now I'm really scared,
It's happening once again.
I know that I am losing
One more of my best friends.

Once, we were inseparable,
We loved to be together,
And I thought I knew for sure
That friends we'd be forever.

I believed it in my heart,
But it looks like I was wrong,
I guess that our relationship
Just wasn't quite that strong.

For it didn't take an argument,
A disagreement or a fight.
At some point we just started
To lead two separate lives.

I know that neither of us wanted
For it to end some day,
But now we're different people,
We're heading different ways.

It hurts so much to go through this
For yet another time,
And it hurts to see that you are fine,
While I'm the one who's crying.

For I'm always thinking back
To the good times that we shared,
Yet you just walk away from them
Like you don't even care.

I've lost so many people
That I've cared about a lot;
So this last scar will rest
With all the others on my heart.

And carefully I'll trust again,
And one day in the end,
My heart will be much stronger
From the pain of losing friends.

♥

Growing Apart and Different

At times I have struggled to avoid letting myself grow apart from certain friends, but the truth is we shouldn't have to struggle so hard to maintain friendships. As time passes, we become different people with diverging interests. Not better or worse people, just different. The people we become don't always mesh with our old friends, and there is nothing worse than forcing a friendship that no longer works. We don't always have to have a falling out to separate ourselves from people— sometimes there's just nothing left.

—COLIN MORTENSEN

A Smile So Genuine

EMILY STARR

To dream of the person you want to be
is a waste of the person you are.

Anonymous

She had been my best friend for over a decade, and when you're sixteen, that's a long time. Every substantial event in my life I'd shared with her, from the sudden death of my grandmother to the cute guy in English asking me what I got on the vocab quiz. There were a million inside jokes that we laughed about and many secrets that strengthened our unbreakable friendship. Even though we shared so much, it was impossible to ignore that we were two very different personalities. It had never occurred to me that our differences could destroy the bonds that had kept us together for so long. It seemed as though our friendship was immune to the terrors that ripped apart other relationships. *We* had something special. *We* were different.

She was much more social than I. She was the type of person who attracted friends with no effort on her part. Guys loved her outgoing spirit and dynamic smile, and girls admired her contagious laughter and the confidence that seemed to radiate from her. I, however, was much more quiet and reserved, and often caught myself staring at her full of envy, while pushing the burning emotions to the back of my mind. Sometimes I wanted to tell people how selfish she really was. I wanted to scream out to everyone that she was lazy, impulsive and undependable, but I couldn't. After all, she *was* my best friend.

Gradually my world started to splinter, and I felt as though I was losing ground. There were so many things to do, and the more I needed her there for me, the more I couldn't find her. She had picked up several new interests earlier that year and developed numerous friendships with people I didn't even know. Then, one unforgettable day, she told me that she didn't want to be best friends anymore. She desperately tried to explain that I was too smart and too intense for her, and that somehow I dragged her down. She pleaded with me not to be mad, but by that time I wasn't listening anymore. I felt as though the floorboards had collapsed from under me and I was plummeting down with them.

We didn't talk after that. I often saw her at school, and we greeted each other with friendly smiles, though mine was practiced and fabricated. She walked the halls surrounded by friends, and I felt like this intense hopelessness had taken over my entire being. I shuddered every time I saw her laugh gaily with the other girls, and I imagined it was all because she was so much happier without me to weigh her down. My other friends had already established close relations amongst themselves; for once I was completely alone. I began to feel like I was a burden to those who knew me. I figured I was a social misfit, and I began avoiding contact with people for fear that I would once again be rejected.

Sometimes when you hold something so close, when you make it the center of your world, it evaporates into thin air and all you have left are the painful memories and the shards of the life that once was. She *was* my life. I had no need to make other friends! I had no need to fit in anywhere else as long as I had her to be there during the hard times and to smile with me during the joyous times. I had lost sight of *me* as an individual and thought only of myself as a package with her. Though it took some time, I made a few new friends that year— people who shared my interests and weren't constantly followed by a mob of adoring fans. I began to like being an individual! I felt replenished having discovered myself for who I was, and not who I pretended to be.

I have learned a lot about myself through that experience. Now that I have discovered who I *really* am, I have a lot more self-respect, as well as adoring fans of my own who do not see me as a weight on their shoulders, but as a nice person who has a lot to offer in a friendship. I still see her in the halls and we smile and wave to each other, only now, my smile is truly genuine.

Evolution of a Friendship

SARAH HUTSON

I was sitting on my floor Sunday afternoon with a huge pile of creased and worn letters in front of me. They were simple notes, passed after class, in class, or between classes, which I had kept for sentimental value—or to indulge my pack-rat instinct. None of the letters had a date on them. We rarely thought beyond the moment when there was just enough time to pass along a juicy bit of gossip, wrapped up in a note and carefully hidden from the omnipresent gaze of the teacher. But it really didn't matter. Just reading the words, "Did you see who was talking to Ben?" or "I can't believe he's going to the dance with that girl!" immediately brought to mind the time and place of the aforementioned incident as if it was stored by guy-of-the-month in a card catalog of memories. And it is quite a collection of memories. We had romance, mystery, horror and, above all, friendship. I still remember how reading the words, "I've got to talk to you!" and "Maybe we can do something this weekend" brought a thrill to my heart—the thrill of knowing you have a best friend.

"Mind if I sit here?"

"No."

"Okay."

Madeline and I met in Home Ec class in the seventh grade. She was quiet and shy, and she wouldn't quite look me in the eye. I was new to the school that year and trying ever so hard to blend in. Madeline looked harmless enough. She had olive skin and dark hair cut short with full bangs. Thick glasses hid the most remarkable green eyes I'd ever seen. We were partnered together in the same kitchenette and we both had our own ideas as to how one should cook. In other words, we constantly bickered and fought—quite an accomplishment considering our timid and self-conscious natures. From that first day, we were comfortable enough with one another to be our disagreeable selves. And with that, a four-year era had begun.

"Are you going to open house at the high school tonight?"

"Yes, are you?"

"Yeah. Will you go with me?"

"Oh good! I was afraid I'd have to go by myself. You know I'd get lost in that place."

Madeline and I did everything together. With the start of high school, our insecurities erupted as violently as did our complexions. Yet we could face anything together. In any situation, we had someone with whom we could talk and hang out. Together we were strong, and together we had confidence. And that simple fact led me to drag Madeline to church every Sunday. My parents and I had just joined a new church, and I knew not one living soul there, so I brought Madeline. Pretty soon everyone in the youth group was as close as peas in a pod, and it was as much Madeline's church as it was mine.

Our sophomore year started out like any other, and by March we both had our driver's licenses and were loving being sixteen. Yet, something began to change between us. We had grown, naturally enough, both physically and mentally. Madeline was now tall and slim. She had grown out her bangs, and her chestnut tresses, glowing with russet highlights, fell in shining waves past her shoulders. But the change was more than just the superficial. I don't know when it started or what caused it, and I wasn't even aware of it at the time, but it was there.

"So, Sarah, what did you do this weekend?"

"Not much. I was working on that project forever."

"Anne, you have no life whatsoever."

"What do you want? I had school work to do and. . . ."

"You see! You are such a goody-good!"

"Get off it! I do things. I just don't do the kind of things you do, Madeline Grace McKineth!"

"Mother Goose, I hate to tell you, but I am *not* your daughter!"

We didn't talk as much anymore. And it seemed we never had enough time for each other. But we were still friends—at least on the surface.

"We might not be able to get together and see each other as much. . . . Some day, in years to come, I hope we will come in contact and not forget about each other as many people do." Signed, "Madeline."

That note, written in my tenth-grade yearbook, was the last one I got from her. We had grown farther and farther apart, and it scared me.

I grieved for our friendship. I went through the shock at first, and was gratefully numb. Then the denial set in, and I pretended things were like they had been. I went through the anger stage next, blaming Maddie for not wanting our friendship to last and myself for caring. It took a while, but finally I realized that a person's needs change; we had grown up together, and in that growing up we had outgrown our need for the other.

Still, it was hard for me. I missed Madeline and how close we used to be. Sitting on my floor, I gradually accepted that we would probably never be friends again. We had planned to room together in college, get an apartment in the city, marry two brothers and live next door to each other. Now it seemed even more ridiculous than when Maddie and I had planned it all out one Friday night, years ago, at four in the morning between smothered giggles and hushes from my parents. Just then the phone rang, interrupting my bittersweet reminiscing, and I reached for it involuntarily.

"Hello, Sarah? It's me, Maddie."

Even Though I Lost a Friend

EMILY BOIVIE

We were always together,
We swore we'd never part.
Where I was, there you were,
Best of friends from the start.
We both looked alike,
With hair and eyes of brown.
When you were happy, I smiled,
When I was upset, you'd frown.
There was only you in my world,
And no one but me in yours.
We shared everything friends could share,
Our music, our clothes, our chores.
Then suddenly this friendship we knew,
Began to change too fast.
The magic of "us" had disappeared,
It was clear this wouldn't last.
We struggled and struggled to save it all,

We were put to the ultimate test.
Then before we knew it, we had both changed,
In the long run, for the best.
We had become two different people,
As our friendship reached great dangers.
The two little girls who were once best friends,
Are now young ladies and strangers.
And for the first time in a while,
I finally feel free.
And even though I lost a friend,
I somehow gained a me.

Eleven

The Best of Friendship

Don't walk in front of me,
I may not follow.
Don't walk behind me,
I may not lead.
Walk beside me and be
my friend.

Albert Camus

The Best of Friendship

I decided to put this chapter at the end of the book because it is important that you finish this book with a celebration of friendship.

As I sit here and think about all the friends I have been blessed to have, it is difficult to say what "the best" of friendship is. I have friends who I have had for many years and friends who I have known for a short while. I have friends I speak to frequently and some that I haven't spoken with in a very long time. The one thing that is present with all of these is this very warm feeling I get when I think of them. I love them. These friendships come in so many different forms and have come from so many different kinds of people. I have friends who are old and friends who are young. I think my greatest happiness has come from the fact that I haven't placed limitations on who or what kind of people I become friends with. So for me the best thing about friendship is that it isn't about age or looks or even shared commonalities, but instead it is about hearts that understand we are all one and the same.

I asked my teenage friends what they thought was the *best* thing about friendship and here are some of their answers:

- "Having someone to talk to and understand you."
  Caitlin Owens
- "You have someone who you can trust and confide in with your deepest secrets and feelings."
  Jenny Sharaf
- "Forgiveness, to a certain extent, keeps a friendship flowing, helping you climb over the walls that mistakes create."
  Cary McCormick
- "The best thing about a good friendship is that you can talk to the person about anything and your friend won't judge you and will support you."
  Ashley Fisher
- "Having someone to share your feelings and secrets with."
  Lily Lamden
- "Security, safety, warmth and trust."
  Emma Bates
- "All the hugs, smiles, laughter and sweet words you absolutely cherish and can't live without."
  Hayley Gibson
- "The best thing about friendship is being able to feel safe and know nothing bad is going to happen when you're with this one person. Being able to know that they always have an open shoulder to cry on, wherever, whenever."
  Vanessa Little
- " 'Cause it's okay when they see you naked."
  Nico Aquayo

Letter to a Friend

SARA RONIS

Dear friend,
I have never told you but
You touched my soul
With sculptor's hands
And molded me into something
    Good
    Kind
    Honest
You are there
To hold my hand
When I'm afraid of me
Who else could I call
With something to say
Only to find
Nothing needs to be said?
If a friend is a gift
You give yourself
I have given myself
The best of presents.

Dear Lauren

KATIE D'ELENA AND LAUREN FARRELL

This letter was given to me the day after my boyfriend of three months broke up with me. I had called my friend Katie crying the night before, and the next morning in school, she handed me this letter. It said, "Miss Lauren" on the front of the envelope and, "Something to make you feel better!! (I hope)" on the back. Every word she wrote is magnificent and I refuse to keep it to myself. I've read it to every friend since then who's been through a tough breakup, whether it was a three-week relationship or a yearlong romance. What Katie wrote in this letter is absolutely true: Friends are forever.

My dearest Lauren,

Hey sweetie! I just got off the phone with you. I wish that I could change things and make them easier for you, but I can't. Happiness is something that will come in time. However, it may come quicker than you think. I know how you feel, considering I was just there myself. However, all breakups are different, so I don't know exactly how you feel. But feel free to tell me at any time.

I'm not going to say that things are going to be okay right away, because they won't. But believe me, your friends will help tremendously. Yep, that's right, no matter what you go through in life, whether guy trouble or parent problems, we will always be there when you need us. And after everything that happened with me, I'd have to say that's the most important lesson I learned. Although I never thought it would end, it did. And when I walked into school the next day, you guys were all there with love, support and flirt certificates. And I felt loved again; I felt special again. Because of you guys I had the strength to make it through that day and all the rest. I hope that this morning you feel the same way. Because Lauren, you are special, you are loved. Regardless of what happens with anybody else, we will always feel that way. Your laughter, smile and awesome personality shine through and make you the Lauren you are. When I'm old and grown, I'll tell my kids about my good friends—not about some guy I went out with. It's you guys who make me the person I am, and I hope that I do the same for you.

I know how alone you feel right now, kind of like you're missing half of you. How are you supposed to live without his touch or his kiss? In time, although you'll always remember him, you'll learn that a hug from a friend is worth thousands of his kisses (even if it isn't the same). I'm not saying that I'm an expert on breaking up, because I'm not. In fact, I wish I didn't know what it was like. But it is truly amazing to realize how much you are loved by your friends. And you feel it in your guts, as weird as it may sound. You actually feel love. And I guess I realized that, although it's a different feeling from what you had with your boyfriend, it still feels incredible.

I'm not going to give you false hopes by telling you that you two will get back together, because I don't know that. But just remember that high school relationships are not just about a guy and a girl, but kind of like their own learning experiences in a way. Just think of everything you've gained from it and how you can apply it to the next time you date someone (and yes, there will be a next time). There are plenty of fish in the sea. I guess that's how you and I have to look at it. Just because this one is over doesn't mean that another can't begin.

Always remember the things that you guys did, the conversations that made you laugh, the times he held you, the places you went and all your inside jokes. Nobody says that we have to forget them; right now they may seem like the happiest times we've ever had. Don't be afraid to let him see you sad—or even happy. And it's okay to talk about it two weeks later.

Just know that no matter what, we love you. And when we say that, we mean it forever, because that's how long we'll all be friends. No matter where life takes us, we'll always have each other. I hope you can take this letter out and read it when you need to. And know that you're not going through this alone, and that although the pain is there now, it won't be there forever. You will get through this and, believe it or not, after all is said and done, you'll come out a stronger person. And when someone you know breaks up with her boyfriend, you can write her *a letter. Just remember: "It's better to have loved and lost than never to have loved at all." And it's the truth, I swear! I love you.*

Your best friend always,
Katie

Best Friend

SARA GOULD

You told me I was good enough
That I deserved a chance
That I should have the courage
To sing, to laugh, to dance
You told me not to care
What other people thought
'Cause you are my best friend
A gift that can't be bought
And now I want to give you
What you always gave to me
Love, friendship, caring
And most important, dignity
But how can I do this
In ways that equal yours
'Cause what I want to give you
Can't be bought in stores
What I want to give you
Is only a simple phrase
It may not seem like very much
But it is in many ways

What I want to give you
Will never pay my due
What I want to give you
Is a simple, kind Thank You.

People Are Different

You and your best friend are different people. You probably are a lot alike in many ways, but you shouldn't have to be exactly alike in all things. You are different kinds of friends to each other and that should be okay. Some people focus most, if not all, of their energy on their friendships. Other people spend most of their time on school or work. Still others try to find a balance somewhere in between. There is no one right way to be a friend; the important thing is that you try your best to be a thoughtful, caring friend.

—KIMBERLY KIRBERGER

We Chose to Be Friends

TASHA BOUCHER

To this day I'm not quite sure what she found so entertaining about climbing up a Dumpster. And she can't remember the exact reason either; she was only four years old. But up the Dumpster she went.

A group of us kids were playing nearby when I heard her screaming. I ran to grab her and, like the mothers who suddenly have enough strength to lift entire cars off their trapped children, my instincts took over. I was her sister and I was only six, but the sight of blood and the sound of her earsplitting screams made me move at a superhuman pace. Without stopping to think, I immediately hijacked a skateboard from one of the other kids, positioned my sister on it and set out as fast as my little legs could travel for the next three blocks. I ran the whole way home, crouching down low enough so that I could push her and keep her balanced on the board at the same time. My leg and arm muscles ached as I navigated the sidewalks shoving that sister-laden board over every crack and rut. I was a big sister on a big mission. I was out of breath as I rounded the final corner to our apartment building. When I reached the stairs, I yelled up to my mom with a scream she claims can still give her chills.

Tawna ended up being fine. I, on the other hand, relished being the hero for a while. Over the years, my mom loved to tell the story of my little sister's rescue. I guess I *had* been pretty resourceful for a six-year-old kid. It was no isolated incident either. She was my first best friend, and I would have done anything for her.

Luckily for me, this devotion went both ways. At my ninth birthday party, my friends and I, with my little sister furiously trying to keep up with us, roller-skated to the top of a steep street in our neighborhood. It bewilders me how much less daunting that "slope" is today, but back then it was a monster. I rolled, no *flew,* down that hill. I felt invincible. Until my skate caught on a pebble and I was launched through the air. The rest is pretty blurry. When I finally landed, Tawna stepped right in and organized my trek to safety. Like ants collectively marching food toward their ant hill, the girls stood me upright and wheeled me all the way home on my skates.

I nearly broke my arm, but I was fine. Tawna was applauded for her fine wheeling skills. She loved the attention but hadn't helped me for that reason. I was her first best friend, and there was no limit to what she would do for me.

Of course, ours was more complicated than the typical friendship. There was that whole imaginary-line-in-the-back-seat-of-the-car thing. You know the one—constructed to keep one's wayward sibling contained *on her side*. There was the hair pulling and name calling, sure. And the pleas for mercy when a tickling match would go on so long it became torture. We even went through a stage whereby we were constantly compelled to try to bite each other's noses off. And then there was my personal favorite threat, "Ooooh . . . I'm gonna *tell*." All to the soundtrack of my parents' repeated cries of, "Knock it off, you two!"

But there were other, kinder moments, too. When we were little and both of us happened to be crying, for instance, one of us would stop and let the other cry. It wasn't like we took turns or anything; we just seemed to naturally figure out who needed to cry more.

I let her borrow my cool clothes (which really weren't so cool now that I look back), and would give her fashion tips since I was convinced she shouldn't go to school representing our good name looking like a Cabbage Patch kid. She would patiently indulge me when I needed to analyze every last gesture of that guy in second period—even though guys still had "cooties" for her.

When I lost my first love she held me tight and told me I would be okay. She wanted to yell and scream at him for hurting me, but didn't. When friends would treat her badly I let her vent her anger and told her it would all work out. I wanted to tell those "friends" a thing or two about friendship, but didn't. When I graduated high school, she cried because she was proud of me—and because she was losing me. When she was crowned Homecoming Queen I smiled because I knew she had finally outgrown that Cabbage Patch look, and because

I wasn't the only one to recognize her inner beauty and quiet strength.

We giggle and dance and dream together. We carry each other's secrets and hold each other's deepest hopes. We pick each other up when we are down and do our best to wheel each other to safety. We have somehow been able to parlay a close sibling bond into a symbiotic friendship, and that makes me so proud. We *had* to be sisters. We *chose* to be friends.

Always

MARIE BLOUIN

You were there for me
When I needed you to be.
When I felt like I had nothing left,
At least nothing I could see.

You were there for me
When he called me on the phone.
The night he made me cry
You wouldn't let me be alone.

You were there for me
Through days, and weeks, and months.
When sadness would befall me
To my side you'd always rush.

You were there for me
When I finally could smile.
I got past all the heartache,
Though it's taken me awhile.

You were there for me always.
When I called for you, you came.
And if ever you should need someone,
You know I'll do the same.

To My Best Friends

DANIELLE GRECO

You have felt everything that I have felt.
You have helped share the hand that I've been dealt.

You have encouraged me in everything that I do.
You have stood up for me, not caring what others
    would think of you.

You have given me advice both good and bad.
You have comforted me when I was sad.

You have respected me for who I am.
You have helped me out by taking my hand.

You have helped me with choices that were hard for me.
You have solved things that I thought were a mystery.

You have been there when I just wanted to talk.
You have colored in the world with just one piece of
    chalk.

You have said the same things I have said.
You have read the same books I have read.

You have done everything for me that you could do.
You have shown to me that you are true.

You have listened to me talk for hours at a time.
You never complained, I never heard you whine.

You have washed away the tears on my face.
You have told me I was special when I felt like a
    disgrace.

You have been, are, and will be my friend.
For all this, my thanks I want to send.

Perfect Memories

ELLARY ALLIS

All my life I waited for the perfect best friend. I always wanted someone to create the perfect childhood memories with, like somehow good memories could heal the bad ones, the dark times of depression. I've had many "best friends" through the years; ones I thought were ideal at the time. The one problem with these friendships? They didn't last. These friendships dissipated along with the quickly fading letters, all with the same message written in childish block letters at the bottom: Best Friends Forever. When you're six you actually believe in forever.

It's almost time for finals, which means my freshman year of high school is winding down. Tonight I came across a picture of Caroline and me wearing wings. I smiled, remembering everything that's happened this year, and the way we've come out of it better friends than ever.

It was chilly in my seaside hometown outside of Los Angeles on the afternoon we first walked to the beach from my house. We were sitting on the floor of my room, eating Häagen-Dazs coffee ice cream, when I spotted the light blue wings from an old Halloween costume lying in a box. I smiled and put them on, claiming that if I were a Hollywood starlet I would start sporting the wings as a new trend. Caroline got up and put on some black feathered angel wings she found in the box. Maybe it was temporary brain freeze from the ice cream that made us do it; whatever it was, we decided to try and walk to the beach, still wearing the wings.

The biggest obstacle we faced was crossing the highway. The zooming cars on the Pacific Coast Highway left us wondering if we were going to make it to the beach alive. We clutched each other's hands and ran screaming across the highway, falling onto the sand to catch our breath when we made it across. It was like a revolution when we arrived at the shore, a realization that we'd made it and there was a whole world outside our own backyards. And it took less than fifteen minutes to get there. We rolled up our Dickies and waded in the water, still wearing our wings; she, the hauntingly beautiful punk rocker angel with a red backwards baseball cap, and me, the glittering gauze-winged fairy who still hadn't stopped believing in Peter Pan. The sunset looked like someone had turned all the colored spotlights of Hollywood across the sky above the ocean.

Caroline and I twirled and cartwheeled across the sand, lost in our own pink and orange glowing world. Suddenly, we noticed that we were being watched. Actually, not just watched, photographed. A woman in a turban had captured us on film. She took her camera away from her face, and smiled at us and shook her head. We grinned and went back to chasing the waves. I had dropped my Tinkerbell watch in the ocean so it had stopped, but the sky was fading into twilight so we figured it was time to go home. As we turned to leave, I took the flower I had picked on the way to the beach out of my hair. Caroline and I walked over and gave it to a man sitting alone by the seashore with his watercolors on his lap. He looked up and smiled, and as we left I turned back to see him lift the flower to his face as the last flash of sunlight slipped away.

We left then, but not for the last time. We continued to walk to the beach after school, relying on the sun to tell us when we should start heading home. We haven't gone for a while, but there's a whole summer of California sunsets ahead of us now. Maybe the photographer and the painter remember an angel and a fairy who once came to dance on the beach together and make memories, which are maybe the only things that will really last forever. If they don't remember us, that's okay. What matters is that *I* remember them. They've become a part of my memories, childhood memories I've shared with Caroline who is, maybe not forever but for the moment anyway, a perfect best friend.

# Resources for Friends in Trouble

Hotlines

800-Suicide: 800-784-2433

Al-Anon/Al-A-Teen: 800-344-2666
For friends and family of people with drinking problems

American Anorexia/Bulimia Association: 212-575-6200
165 W. 46th Street, #1108, New York, NY 10036
Confidential and free referrals and resources

Boys Town National Hotline: 800-448-3000
Bilingual suicide prevention hotline for boys and girls

Bulimia/Anorexia Self-Help Hotline: 800-227-4785

Center for Substance Abuse Treatment: 800-662-HELP
(Web site: *www.adp.cahwnet.gov*)

Children of the Night: 800-551-1300
(Web site: *www.childrenofthenight.org*)
Rescuing America's children from the ravages of street
prostitution

Covenant House Nine Line: 800-999-9999
(Web site: *www.covenanthouse.org*)
Youth crisis hotline for talking about any problem

Kid Save: 800-543-7283
Gives information and referrals to kids in crisis

National AIDS Hotline: 800-342-2437
(Web site: *www.ashastd.org*)

National Child Abuse Hotline: 800-422-4453
(Web site: *www.childhealthusa.org*)

National Runaway Switchboard: 800-621-4000
(E-mail: *info@nrscrisisline.org*)

Teen AIDS Hotline: 800-234-4-TEEN

Yellow Ribbon Project: 303-429-3530, 3531, 3532
(Web site: *www.yellowribbon.org*)
Helps prevent teen suicide

Youth Crisis Hotline: 800-448-4663
No problem is too big or too small

Web Sites

American Association of Suicidology: *www.suicidology.org*

Befrienders International: *www.befrienders.org*
International referral service for suicide prevention

CARING: *www.caringonline.org*
Provides automated healthcare information

Eating Disorder Recovery Online: *www.edrecovery.com*

Eating Disorders Awareness and Prevention, Inc.:
www.edap.org

Gay, Bi or Questioning Teens: *www.outproud.org*
They may have the answers you're searching for

Narcotics Anonymous: *www.na.org*
When you need help with drugs

Rape and Incest (RAINN): *www.rainn.org*
Started by Tori Amos, herself a survivor of rape

SA/VE (Suicide Awareness/Voices of Education):
www.save.org

TEEN LINE: *www.teenlineonline.org*

Violence Resources: *www.child.net / violence.htm*
Just one call can end a problem

Suggested Reading

Are You There God? It's Me, Margaret by Judy Blume (Yearling). A coming-of-age story told through the eyes of a twelve-year-old.

The Bell Jar by Sylvia Plath (Bantam Books). The classic autobiographical novel about a young woman's mental breakdown.

Deal With It! A Whole New Approach to Your Body, Brain and Life as a Gurl by Esther Drill, Heather McDonald and Rebecca Odes (Pocket Books).

Girl, Interrupted by Susanna Kaysen (Vintage Books). A riveting tale of how the author was hospitalized while growing up because she refused to conform.

Go Ask Alice by Anonymous (Aladdin Paperbacks). A painfully honest account of a fifteen-year-old girl's harrowing experience with drugs, written in diary form.

Letters to My Son: A Father's Wisdom on Manhood, Women, Life and Love by Kent Nerburn (New World Library).

Ophelia Speaks: Adolescent Girls Write About Their Search for Self by Sara Shandler (HarperCollins).

Prozac Nation by Elizabeth Wurtzel (Riverhead Books). A twentysomething woman's memoir of her battles with depression and drugs.

Reviving Ophelia: Saving the Selves of Adolescent Girls by Mary Pipher (Ballantine Books).

Surviving High School by Michael Riera (Celestial Arts). Helps readers make positive decisions for themselves.

TeenInk: Our Voices, Our Visions by John and Stephanie
Meyer (HCI Teens). Teenagers sharing their thoughts on
friends, family, fitting in, challenges, loss, memories, love and
heroes.

Wasted: A Memoir of Anorexia and Bulimia by Marya
Hornbacher (HarperCollins). A passionate and eloquent
account of a young woman's near-death self-starvation.

For Your Parents:

Uncommon Sense for Parents with Teenagers by Michael
Riera (Celestial Arts).

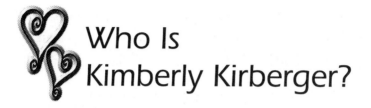

Who Is
Kimberly Kirberger?

Kimberly is an advocate for teens, a writer for teens, a mother of a teen, and a friend and confidante to the many teens in her life. She is committed to bettering the lives of teens around the globe through her books and the outreach she does for teens on behalf of her organization, Inspiration and Motivation for Teens, Inc.

Kim's love for teens was first expressed globally with the publication of the bestselling *Chicken Soup for the Teenage Soul*. This book was a true labor of love for Kim, and the result of years of friendship and research with teens from whom she learned what really matters. After the success of the first *Teenage Soul* book, and the outpouring of hundreds and thousands of letters and submissions from teens around the world, Kim went on to coauthor the *New York Times* #1 bestsellers *Chicken Soup for the Teenage Soul II* and *Chicken Soul for the Teenage Soul III*, *Chicken Soup for the Teenage Soul Journal* and *Chicken Soup for the College Soul*. She is currently at work on the upcoming *Chicken Soup for the Teenage Soul Letters*.

In October 1999, the first book in Kim's *Teen Love* series was released. *Teen Love: On Relationships* has since become a *New York Times* bestseller and the inspiration behind her popular Web site, *www.love4teens.com*. Her friendship and collaboration with Colin Mortensen of MTV's *Real World Hawaii* produced the much-loved *Teen Love: A Journal on Relationships*.

Kim's empathic understanding of the issues affecting parents led her to coauthor the recent release *Chicken Soul for the Parent's Soul*. She is also currently working on a book for both parents and teens that she hopes will give both sides of this relationship the support they need.

Kim lives in Southern California with her husband, John, and son, Jesse. When she is not reading letters she gets from teens, she is offering them support and encouragement in the forums on her Web site, *www.teenagechickensoup.com*. She also enjoys nurturing her family, listening to her son's band and hanging out with her son's friends when they will let her.

Kimberly can be reached at:

I.A.M. for Teens, Inc.
P.O. Box 936, Pacific Palisades, CA 90272
www.teenagechickensoup.com
or
www.love4teens.com
e-mail for stories: *stories@teenagechickensoup.com*
e-mail for letters and feedback for the *Teen Love* series:
kim@love4teens.com

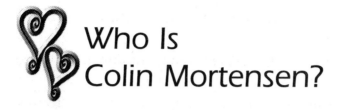 Who Is Colin Mortensen?

Colin Mortensen is a twenty-year-old actor/writer currently living in Los Angeles, California.

After graduating from high school, Colin completed two years of studies at the University of California at Berkeley at the top of his class. During his time at Berkeley, Colin not only excelled academically, but also was heavily involved with the campus television and radio stations and the theater community, honing his writing and performing skills and launching his career as an on-air personality.

While attending Berkeley, Colin auditioned for and was chosen as the host of MTV's *Real World/Road Rules Casting Special,* his television debut. Based on the exuberant reception of his breakout performance on the casting special, Colin was chosen as the first cast member of MTV's *Real World Hawaii* (MTV's highest-rated series ever) and was later voted its most popular cast member.

After completing filming for the *Real World,* Colin moved to Los Angeles in order to pursue his passion for acting. Once in Los Angeles, he was immediately cast as the sexy, clueless office assistant, AJ, in the critically acclaimed NBC comedy *MYOB,* written and created by

Don Roos. An NBC "summer hit," *MYOB* received excellent ratings.

Following his MTV fame and his role on *MYOB,* Colin hit the cover of *TV Guide* and was soon after chosen as one of E-Online's "Sizzlin' Sixteen," one of eight male actors predicted to be up-and-coming stars (former E-Online selections include Matt Damon, Ben Affleck and Joaquin Phoenix). Shortly after, in a *TV Guide* poll of millions of fans and viewers, Colin was voted "the sexiest *Real World* cast member of all time."

In December 1999, Colin became a published writer with the release of *Teen Love: A Journal on Relationships.* Colin's words of wisdom from the "guy's point of view" lend a fresh voice to the first journal in Kimberly Kirberger's *Teen Love* series.

Colin not only devotes himself to a rigorous acting and writing schedule, he also remains committed to young people about various issues that concern them and affect their lives. Colin believes that being in the "public eye" offers him a unique opportunity to present young adults with healthy, positive messages and advice. He enjoys sharing his experiences and perspectives to packed auditoriums of supportive fans.

Colin is dedicated to the creative passions in his life: writing, acting and making a difference in the world.

Contributors

Natalie Abel is a seventeen-year-old senior from Grenada, Mississippi, where she is a varsity cheerleader, drum major of the school band, vice president of the student council and a member of the National Honor Society. She is a member of First Baptist Church and is active in her youth group. She can be reached at *jabel@dixie-net.com*.

Ellary Allis lives in Pacific Palisades, California, and is a fifteen-year-old sophomore in high school. She loves singing and photography, but writing is how she most clearly expresses herself. She wrote her story at Mameson Ranch Camp, where she spent the summer. She can be reached at *Firefly018@aol.com*.

Lindsey Ataya is a seventeen-year-old student in Victoria, B.C., Canada. She is a member of her school's basketball and fastball teams, and enjoys snowboarding and working out. She finds that writing helps to deal with the stress in her life, and hopes to someday become a successful writer. She can be reached at *lindzed10@icqmail.com*.

Natalie Baltzley is a high school student in Des Moines, Iowa. She enjoys writing for the school newspaper, acting in plays, going to the local hockey games, spending time with friends, reading and listening to music. She hopes to attend Yale or Columbia after high school. Natalie can be reached at *Noodely21@aol.com*.

Marie Blouin is a senior high school student in Ontario, Canada. She enjoys playing guitar, listening to music, photography and writing poems. This is her first published work, and she is thankful to God and her family and friends who have always been there for her. This is dedicated to them. She can be reached at *marieb83@hotmail.com*.

Emily Boivie is a student and an aspiring actress. She enjoys writing, music and drama. She would like to dedicate this poem to her sister and inspiration, Ilana. She would also like to thank Mike, her family and all her wonderful friends. She can be reached at *emboivie@yahoo.com*.

Jenny Bokoch lives in Encinitas, California, with her mom, dad, and sister, Rebecca. She is currently a sophomore in high school. Jenny would like to thank her friends, family and teachers for always supporting her writing and for giving her the confidence to succeed.

Tasha Boucher lives in Los Angeles and is a graduate student in the Counseling program at Cal State Northridge. She has worked as a counselor with at-risk teens and currently teaches a Creative Writing workshop to teenage girls in residential treatment. Her greatest joy has come from her relationship with an incredible teenage girl she has had the pleasure of mentoring over the past three years. Tasha can be reached at *tasha_boucher@hotmail.com*.

Ryan Bove is a writer from Pittsburgh. He is currently enrolled as a ninth-grader in high school. He has accumulated numerous writing accolades. Ryan has been published in many newspapers and magazines. He also earned third place in a national writing competition. Ryan can be reached at *rmb02@hotmail.com*.

Allie Busby has written more stories, but "Christy" is the first to be published. It is dedicated to one of her closest friends, Stacy. Allie can be reached at *strwbrykisd@excite.com*.

Jenna Butrenchuk is a student at the University of Lethbridge. She has published a few minor prose and poetry pieces to date. This story is dedicated to Jennifer Scott. Jenna can be reached at *jbutrenchuk @telusplanet.net*.

Noah Campana is a college student who lives on the Olympic Peninsula in Washington. He loves to write and wants to be a writer. This story is dedicated to Bre. Noah can be reached at *grampus_orca @hotmail.com*.

Jennifer Carden is nineteen years old and currently in her sophomore year of college. She is studying to be a Christian schoolteacher. Jennifer has loved to write poetry and short stories for as long as she can remember. She dedicates this poem to her family, who have always been there encouraging her to write. She can be reached at *jennyal81@hotmail.com*.

Melissa Collette is a nineteen-year-old college student pursuing a career in film and television and elementary education. Her poem "Inside" appears in *Chicken Soup for the Teenage Soul II*. She would like to thank all of the many inspired teens who have written to her to share their own stories of heartbreak and recovery. Melissa would really love for you to e-mail her at *huneebee17@yahoo.com.*

Alison Dankmeyer is a spirited eighteen-year-old about to begin university life in Ontario, Canada. She writes a weekly column for her town newspaper and has remained very active throughout high school. She writes mostly for herself and friends, but one day hopes to publish her very own book. Alison can be reached at *starbo81@hotmail.com.*

Crystal Davis is a seventeen-year-old senior from Foyil, Oklahoma. She enjoys writing poetry and short stories and has had poems published in various anthologies. She can be reached at *valleygrl00@hotmail.com.*

Jennifer "Micki" Davison was born in Augsburg, Bavaria, West Germany. She now lives in Olalla, Washington, where she is in the eighth grade. She attributes her love for writing, reading and poetry to two special teachers, Mrs. Sunny Willson and Mr. Kaye, as well as her mother, her brother, Chris, and the support of her best friends, Jessica Elliott and James Dillard. She can be reached at *skfreak@hotmail.com.*

Katie D'Elena is an eighteen-year-old senior. She is excited about her publication and hopes that her letter will offer the same comfort she has found through other *Teen Love* stories. She dedicates this letter to all her friends for always making the bad times better and the good times wonderful memories. She can be reached at *Kate101282@aol.com.*

Alice Dodds is seventeen and has lived her whole life in a suburb outside of Boston. Her second-grade teacher got her interested in poetry, and ever since then she has never stopped writing. She wrote "Lollipop Days" when she was fifteen. Although she has had two other poems published, this is her first experience with a major publication. She dedicates this poem to friendship, and to all the friends she has now, as well as to all of the friends she has lost along the way. She can be reached at *AliKat1982@aol.com.*

Jessica Dowdy is currently in the Class of 2001 at her high school in La Grande, Oregon. As an outgoing athlete, friend, daughter, sister and peer, she experiences "life's little surprises" every day. Jessica loves volleyball and hopes to continue pursuing her career at the collegiate level. She also enjoys traveling, swimming, spending time with friends, writing and the beach. She encourages anyone to contact her at: *jldowdy24@yahoo.com.*

Mollie F. Drabik is fourteen years old and resides in Little Canada, Minnesota, with her parents, Claudia and Hank, and her brother, Mike. She enjoys many sports and anything that has to do with art. "Gold Friend" is about her friend, Lindsey. Mollie is looking forward to high school this fall.

Carol Elaine Faivre-Scott is a former newspaper reporter and radio news director. She now owns an Internet service providership in partnership with her husband and their friend. The mother of four children, and also a four-time grandma, she occasionally finds time to write freelance poetry and short articles. She can be reached at *carol@next-wave.net*.

Lauren Farrell is currently a senior in high school. She enjoys the summer, the company of her family and friends, and acting, a hobby she plans on pursuing further in the future. She thanks her amazing friends for always being there because without them she wouldn't be nearly as much fun! Lauren can be reached at *tinkerbell514@hotmail.com*.

Chrissy Farwell is a high school student in ninth grade. She likes to sing, write and draw, and hopes to one day be famous! She can be reached at *sexay_dudette@hotmail.com*.

Kate Florig is sixteen years old and will be a junior in high school in the fall of 2000. Ever since the incident depicted in her story, her friends have become an even larger part of her life and without their support she would be a completely different person. Kate can be reached at *k8angel15@yahoo.com*.

Lia Gay is currently a junior at the University of Kansas. She enjoys writing and has contributed to all three books in the *Chicken Soup for the Teenage Soul* series. She wishes to dedicate this story to all of the friends who have touched her life, including her family, and James, too!

Randy Glasbergen has had more than twenty-five thousand cartoons published in magazines, books and greeting cards around the world. He also creates *The Better Half*, which is syndicated to newspapers by King Features Syndicate. You can find more of Randy's cartoons online at *www.glasbergen.com*.

Danielle Glickson is a fifteen-year-old attending ninth grade. She enjoys dancing, reading poetry, writing, spending time with her girl-friends and participating in regular teenage social gatherings. She can be reached through e-mail at *DUNYA1@worldnet.att.net*.

Sara Gould is thirteen and a seventh-grader from Simsbury, Connecticut. In her spare time Sara enjoys playing soccer on her local travel team and shopping. Sara wishes to dedicate her poem to all of her friends who have helped her through the years.

Taylor Gramps is a high school student. She writes for the school paper, *The Standard,* and the school's literary magazine, *Indelible Ink.* She enjoys writing, acting, singing, chatting with friends, watching movies and listening to music. Taylor thanks her best friends and family for their undying love and support. Taylor can be reached at *Tate4765@aol.com.*

Danielle Greco is fourteen years old. She is an eighth-grade student in Pittsburgh, Pennsylvania. This is her first published poem, and she hopes that she can publish more in the future. Danielle dedicates this poem to Caitlin Ambrose, Mallory Anderson and Shannon McGeorge. She can be reached at *iiiangel75@aol.com.*

Tracey R. Grimm is a junior in high school from Chesapeake, Virginia. She plays softball, writes poetry, competes in forensics and is an editor for her school newspaper. She hopes to one day rule the world. This poem is dedicated to Rose and Anna. She can be reached at *unsugarless@hotmail.com.*

Rebecca Heydon is a high school student in New Jersey. She likes to write and would love to work in that field some day. She loves gymnastics and lacrosse. This story is dedicated to all her friends that she has ever had because they all have left some kind of footprint on her heart. She can be reached at *LestatsAngel@aol.com.*

Sarah Hutson is a junior at Campbell University in North Carolina. She is an English Education major and is currently looking into graduate schools. This story is her first published work. She can be reached at *theprincessofquitealot1@juno.com.*

Allison Ice is fifteen and lives in Arizona. She enjoys reading, writing, shopping and spending time with her friends and family. Bible studies and youth group activities are also important to her. She hopes to become a writer or editor someday.

Carmen Johnson is sixteen. She loves chocolate, her bed, the beach, music and being published. She would like to thank her goofy parents. She can be reached at *crjohnson83@hotmail.com.*

Brittany Kusserow is an eighth-grade student from Warsaw, Indiana. She has won second and third place in a writing contest in her hometown and has been to the area's Young Authors Contest three times. She can be reached at *squirrel_girl_123@hotmail.com.*

Christine Leggett is a sophomore studying elementary education, special education and communications at Keene State College in New Hampshire. She looks forward to becoming an elementary school teacher. This letter is dedicated to all her close friends and family, whom she loves with all her heart. She can be reached at *c0okieM@aol.com.*

Justine Lescroart is a junior high school student in Davis, California. She has previously published three poems. Justine's hobbies include reading, horseback riding, skiing and spending time with her friends. This poem is dedicated to all of her friends, the "coffee-house kids," and, of course, to Koo.

Silas Lesnick recently graduated from Sherwood High School in Sandy Spring, Maryland and is currently pursuing film studies at the College of Santa Fe. An avid science fiction fan and comic collector, he also writes and illustrates his own graphic tales. He can be reached at *bee_czar@yahoo.com.*

Rachel Littler is currently a junior in high school in Washington State. She is a dedicated student who is also actively involved in sports, music and church youth group. She thanks the Lord for the inspiration and ability He has blessed her with.

Marisa Marciano is an eleventh-grade student from Woodbridge, Ontario, Canada. She has participated in numerous short story and speech competitions, and continues to write about her life experiences. This story is dedicated to her dearest friend, Marijka Haines, whom she misses more and more every day. She can be reached at *marisa_marciano@hotmail.com.*

Nellie McDowell lives in the rural west Texas town of Imperial, with her husband, Ron, and their children, Cory, Steven and Roni Kay. She has been writing for as long as she can remember, and just recently learned that there were other people out there who actually liked reading some of what she writes. She dedicates this poem to her friends who, through the years, have kept her from "falling apart."

Tannia Millen is a tenth-grade student from Barrie, Ontario, Canada. She enjoys white-water rafting, rock climbing and working with children. She can be reached at *day57@yahoo.com.*

Peggy Miller attends Miami University where she is a member of the campus Fitness Club, as well as the softball team. Peggy volunteers as an assistant coach for a local high school swim team. She also is a twelve-year pianist, volunteers at church and works summers as a lifeguard and swim instructor. Her story is dedicated to Susan and Sadie with love and thanks for their inspiration and encouragement. Peggy can be reached at *peggumsb@yahoo.com.*

Danielle Mortag attends high school in Grafton, Wisconsin. She is vice president of her sophomore class. She is also on the dance team, which has given her the opportunity to travel to Hawaii and Florida. She loves music, poetry and dancing. Danielle can be reached at *destinychica@hotmail.com.*

Dan "Rudy" Mulhausen has just graduated from Southridge High in Kennewick, Washington. He's currently planning to attend the University of Oregon. He also has had a story about his life selected for the upcoming book *Chicken Soup for the Teenage Soul Letters.* He can be reached at *Rudy63@aol.com.*

Becca Mustard, seventeen, is a senior in high school in Thornton, Colorado, where she is the editor-in-chief of her school newspaper. In her spare time, Becca enjoys snowboarding, listening to music and singing, and spending time in the beautiful Colorado Rockies. Becca can be reached at *skabamie@yahoo.com.*

Laurie Nuck, a teacher in southern Monterey County, resides in King City, California, with her husband, Tom. She got her Bilingual Teaching degree at Boise State University. Her writings include "The Magic of Family Literacy" published in *Portals,* an international reading journal, in 1995, and "The Popcorn Can" published in Kay Allenbaugh's *Chocolate for a Lover's Heart,* in 1999. She can be reached at *Bunya@redshift.com.*

Aja Ofte is an eighth grader from Richmond, Virginia. She enjoys writing stories and poetry, singing and playing the piano. She lives with her mom, stepdad and the family cat, Delilah. She is active in her church youth group and is looking forward to a mission trip to Costa Rica in the summer of 2000. She can be reached at *jlimb@richmond.infi.net.*

Carrie Sue O'Maley is a student at Butler University where she studies journalism and English. Her love for writing was encouraged and instilled by her grandma and mom, both accomplished authors. "Holding On to the Gold" is dedicated to Carrie's late rabbit, Henry Buns, as well as Sue Payer Beeghly. Carrie can be reached at *Venuschic4@aol.com.*

Kathy Peterson is a junior in high school from Maysville, Kentucky. She is an honor roll student, an active member of Y-Club, FCCLA, Champions Against Drugs, FCA, NHS, Beta Club, 4-H and Girl Scouts. She also enjoys dancing, public speaking and reading. This is Kathy's first publication.

John Pham is an amateur writer who resides in Pomona, California. Although he writes frequently, this is his first major publication. His hobbies include tennis, reading and, of course, writing. Richard Wright and J.R.R. Tolkien are among his favorite writers. This story is for all those people who had something good, but failed to capitalize on it. John can be reached at *deceptakhan@yahoo.com.*

Natalie Pittsford is a high school junior in Austin, Texas. For her, writing is good therapy. This piece won first prize in a Diversity Week contest at her high school in 1997. She hopes that it will speak to many other young adults and give them courage.

Candy Rhodes was born and raised in North Carolina, where she is a sophomore in high school. She is fifteen years old. Candy enjoys writing stories and poetry, and being with her friends. She can be reached at *candycane213@hotmail.com.*

Sara Ronis is a sixteen-year-old honors student from Montreal. She enjoys reading, hanging out with her friends, dancing and volunteer work. This is her first published story but she has been writing stories and poetry since she was eight. She can be reached at *sara@onsager. chem.mcgill.ca.*

Megan Kimm Snook is a twenty-year-old native Montanan who loves everything connected to the written and spoken word. She would like to extend tremendous thanks to her family for their unfailing support. This piece is dedicated to her dear friend and kindred spirit, Edit Sammel. Megan can be reached at *bluepool@hotmail.com.*

Emily Starr is a sophomore in high school in Claremont, California. She plays varsity basketball and is an active peer counselor and conflict manager on her high school campus. Her all-time favorite book is *Gone with the Wind* by Margaret Mitchell because she admires Scarlett's courage and independence.

Erin Stevens is a high school freshman in New York. She hopes to pursue writing as a career one day. Besides writing, Erin is involved in many other activities such as Model United Nations Club, her school newspaper and the varsity swim team. She would like to thank the characters of the story, her Earth Science class, her parents and the rest of her friends not included in the story.

Laura Tanguay is in her second year at the University of Manitoba, majoring in social work. She hopes to work with children and their families after graduating. She spends her spare time volunteering, reading and playing music. She can be reached at *lauralynn10@yahoo.com*.

Emilie Tani is a high school student in Cupertino, California. She would like to thank all the people at Los Altos United Methodist Church for their continued support and inspiration. This is her first published work and she is extremely excited to share her words. She can be reached at *lmo3566@aol.com*.

Kim Taranto is a future college student hoping to major in English. She writes short stories and poems in her spare time with the hope of someday being a great writer. This poem is dedicated to Robea Patrowicz for her lasting support and friendship.

Roger Todaro is twenty-one years old and will be a freshman at the University of Wisconsin—Stevens Point. He is an aspiring writer who has been writing poetry since he was sixteen and has recently moved on to short stories and song lyrics. This will be his first published piece, and he would like to dedicate it to all his friends whom he loves dearly and will always keep close to his heart.

Jamie Tucker is a nineteen-year-old African-American female living in New Jersey. She has enjoyed writing poetry and fiction since grammar school and would like to thank her mom, family, teachers and special friends for their support and encouragement over the years. Aside from writing, she is interested in a wide variety of music, as well as movies, photography, psychology, animals and computers. Jamie can be reached at *PurtyBrownize@aol.com*.

Heather VanHoose is a high school senior in South Carolina and has already written well over two thousand poems. She has been published in an international literary magazine called Slugfest, Ltd. This poem is dedicated to people who are different, because who really wants to be the same? She can be reached at *GodsLyric@YesIBelieve.com*.

Tal Vigderson lives in Los Angeles and is currently working as an entertainment attorney representing talent, production companies and new media clients. He has had past careers in photography, entertainment-marketing research and teaching. Tal likes to travel and enjoys tennis, writing, hiking and photography. He can be reached at *TOV3@aol.com*.

Sarah Walcott-Sapp is a sophomore in high school. She enjoys running cross-country and track (and is looking forward to learning how to pole vault), playing basketball and spending time with her friends. This is her first poem to be published, and she wants to thank her friends for inspiring her writing.

Becky Welzenbach is a freshman in high school who lives in Arlington Heights, Illinois. She has written since first grade, and attended the Young Authors Conference in 1998 when she was in seventh grade. This poem was written in 1999 for the "Reflections" contest, where it went to the state level. She would like to dedicate this to all her friends, especially Kels, Keds and Robbie. Remember . . . stay solidified!

Kayla Joanna Woods is a sixteen-year-old high school student in Virginia. This is her first story to be published. She wrote this story in her ninth-grade English class. This story really describes the way Kayla thinks and feels. She can be reached at *blondie16_2002_99@yahoo.com*.

Rebecca Woolf is a freelance writer who has been published in *Chicken Soup for the Teenage Soul II* and *III,* as well as *Teen Love: On Relationships.* Rebecca is currently working on publishing her first solo book of poetry called *Broken Mirrors: A Reflective Memoir.* Rebecca has appeared as a guest on MSNBC, CBS and Fox Family, and speaks regularly to students about the importance of writing. Rebecca would like to thank Kim Kirberger for all of the brilliant opportunity she has given so selflessly. (Thank you!) To reach Rebecca, please e-mail her at *rebeccawoolf@leadthestar.com*.

Alexandra Zissu is a writer living in New York City. She has written for the *New York Observer,* the *New York Times,* the *Industry Standard, Self, Cosmopolitan, Harper's Bazaar* and *US Weekly,* among other publications. She can be reached at *lexyzissu@aol.com*.

 Permissions